Praise for the Osborne New Testament Commentaries

"With this new series, readers will have before them what we—his students—experienced in all of Professor Osborne's classes: patient regard for every word in the text, exegetical finesse, a preference for an eclectic resolution to the options facing the interpreter, a sensitivity to theological questions, and most of all a reverence for God's word."

—**Scot McKnight**, Julius R. Mantey Chair of New Testament,
Northern Seminary

"The Osborne New Testament Commentaries draw from the deep well of a lifetime of serious study and teaching. They present significant interpretive insights in a highly accessible, spiritually nurturing format. This is a tremendous resource that will serve a new generation of Bible readers well for years to come. Highly recommended!"

—**Andreas J. Köstenberger**, founder, Biblical Foundations; senior research
professor of New Testament and biblical theology,
Southeastern Baptist Theological Seminary

"Like many others in the church and academy, I have greatly benefitted from the writings of Grant Osborne over the course of my professional career. Grant has a gift for summarizing the salient points in a passage and making clear what he thinks the text means—as well as making it relevant and applicable to believers at all levels of biblical maturity. I especially commend the usefulness of these verse-by-verse commentaries for pastors and lay leaders."

—**Stanley E. Porter**, president, dean, professor of New Testament, and
Roy A. Hope Chair in Christian Worldview, McMaster Divinity College

"For years I have found Grant Osborne's commentaries to be reliable and thoughtful guides for those wanting to better understand the New Testament. Indeed, Osborne has mastered the art of writing sound, helpful, and readable commentaries and I am confident that this new series will continue the level of excellence that we have come to expect from him. How exciting to think that pastors, students, and laity will all be able to benefit for years to come from the wise and insightful interpretation provided by Professor Osborne in this new series. The Osborne New Testament Commentaries will be a great gift for the people of God."

—**David S. Dockery**, president, Trinity International University

"One of my most valued role models, Grant Osborne is a first-tier biblical scholar who brings to the text of Scripture a rich depth of insight that is both accessible and devotional. Grant loves Christ, loves the word, and loves the church, and those loves are embodied in this wonderful new commentary series, which I cannot recommend highly enough."

—**George H. Guthrie**, Benjamin W. Perry Professor of Bible,
Union University

"Grant Osborne is ideally suited to write a series of concise commentaries on the New Testament. His exegetical and hermeneutical skills are well known, and anyone who has had the privilege of being in his classes also knows his pastoral heart and wisdom."

—**Ray Van Neste**, professor of biblical studies, director of the R.C. Ryan Center for Biblical Studies, Union University

"Grant Osborne is an eminent New Testament scholar and warm-hearted professor who loves the word of God. Through decades of effective teaching at Trinity Evangelical Divinity School and church ministry around the world, he has demonstrated an ability to guide his readers in a careful understanding of the Bible. The volumes in this accessible commentary series help readers understand the text clearly and accurately. But they also draw us to consider the implications of the text, providing key insights on faithful application and preaching that reflect a lifetime of ministry experience. This unique combination of scholarship and practical experience makes this series an invaluable resource for all students of God's word, and especially those who are called to preach and teach."

—**H. Wayne Johnson**, associate academic dean and associate professor of pastoral theology, Trinity Evangelical Divinity School

JAMES

Verse by Verse

JAMES

Verse by Verse

GRANT R. OSBORNE

LEXHAM PRESS

James: Verse by Verse
Osborne New Testament Commentaries

Copyright 2019 Grant R. Osborne

Lexham Press, 1313 Commercial St., Bellingham, WA 98225

LexhamPress.com

Print ISBN: 9781683592938
Digital ISBN: 9781683592945

Lexham Editorial Team: Elliot Ritzema, Jeff Reimer, Sarah Awa
Cover Design: Christine Christophersen
Typesetting: ProjectLuz.com

CONTENTS

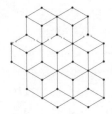

SERIES PREFACE

There are two authors of every biblical book: the human author who penned the words, and the divine Author who revealed and inspired every word. While God did not dictate the words to the biblical writers, he did guide their minds so that they wrote their own words under the influence of the Holy Spirit. If Christians really believed what they said when they called the Bible "the word of God," a lot more would be engaged in serious Bible study. As divine revelation, the Bible deserves, indeed demands, to be studied deeply.

This means that when we study the Bible, we should not be satisfied with a cursory reading in which we insert our own meanings into the text. Instead, we must always ask what God intended to say in every passage. But Bible study should not be a tedious duty we have to perform. It is a sacred privilege and a joy. The deep meaning of any text is a buried treasure; all the riches are waiting under the surface. If we learned there was gold deep under our backyard, nothing would stop us from getting the tools we needed to dig it out. Similarly, in serious Bible study all the treasures and riches of God are waiting to be dug up for our benefit.

This series of commentaries on the New Testament is intended to supply these tools and help the Christian understand more deeply the God-intended meaning of the Bible. Each volume walks the reader verse-by-verse through a book with the goal of opening up for us what God led Matthew or Paul or John to say to their readers. My goal in this series is to make sense of the historical and literary background of these ancient works, to supply the information that will enable the modern reader to understand exactly what the biblical writers were saying to their first-century audience. I want to remove the complexity of most modern commentaries and provide an easy-to-read explanation of the text. I have read nearly all the recent literature and have tried to supply a commentary that sums up the state of knowledge attained to date on the meaning and background for each biblical book.

But it is not enough to know what the books of the New Testament meant back then; we need help in determining how each text applies to our lives today. It is one thing to see what Paul was saying to his readers in Rome or Philippi, and quite another thing to see the significance of his words for us. So at key points in the commentary, I will attempt to help the reader discover areas in our modern lives that the text is addressing.

I envision three main uses for this series:

1. **Devotional Scripture reading.** Many Christians read rapidly through the Bible for devotions in a one-year program. That is extremely helpful to gain a broad overview of the Bible's story. But I strongly encourage another kind of devotional reading—namely, to study deeply a single segment of the biblical text and try to understand it. These commentaries are designed to enable that. The commentary is based on the NIV and explains the meaning of the verses, enabling the modern reader to read a few pages at a time and pray over the message.

2. **Church Bible studies.** I have written these commentaries also to serve as guides for group Bible studies. Many Bible

studies today consist of people coming together and sharing what they think the text is saying. There are strengths in such an approach, but also weaknesses. The problem is that God inspired these scriptural passages so that the church would understand and obey *what he intended the text to say*. Without some guidance into the meaning of the text, we are prone to commit heresy. At the very least, the leaders of the Bible study need to have a commentary so they can guide the discussion in the direction God intended. In my own church Bible studies, I have often had the class read a simple exposition of the text so they can all discuss the God-given message, and that is what I hope to provide here.

3. ***Sermon aids.*** These commentaries are also intended to help pastors faithfully exposit the text in a sermon. Busy pastors often have too little time to study complex thousand-page commentaries on biblical passages. As a result, it is easy to spend little time in Bible study and thereby to have a shallow sermon on Sunday. As I write this series, I am drawing on my own experience as a pastor and interim pastor, asking myself what I would want to include in a sermon.

Overall, my goal in these commentaries is simple: I would like them to be interesting and exciting adventures into New Testament texts. My hope is that readers will discover the riches of God that lie behind every passage in his divine word. I hope every reader will fall in love with God's word as I have and begin a similar lifelong fascination with these eternal truths!

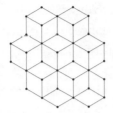

INTRODUCTION TO JAMES

James is probably the first New Testament work to have been written and one of the most fascinating, unique letters ever written. As we will see, it was produced in the early to mid-forties, toward the end of the Jewish-Christian period and just before Paul began his Gentile mission, which would produce the universal church made up of Jews and Gentiles together. James's letter would be remarkably similar in places to the Wisdom literature of the Old Testament, concerned with the conduct of God's people as illustrating divine wisdom.

This has always been a popular book in the church because it is immensely practical and covers so many critical as well as comforting issues like trials and suffering, the proper use of the tongue, and poverty and wealth. On these issues, James's advice exemplifies the wisdom for which this letter is justly famous. Still, for all its popular appeal, it has often been neglected and even maligned because it lacks the kind of deep theology Paul's letters contain. Martin Luther considered removing it from the canon because of the absence of **christological**[1] thought in it. Others have thought

---

1. Terms in bold type are discussed in the glossary (page 177).

it too practical and not sufficiently theoretical to deserve attention, and still others have doubted whether it belongs in the New
Testament because of the absence of its early affirmation among
the church fathers.[2]

James is the one writing we have from the Jewish Christianity
of Jerusalem and surrounding environs before the universal mission and Gentile incursion began. It is of enormous value in helping us to understand the thinking and perspective of that early
period when the church called itself "the Way" (Acts 9:2; 19:9, 23;
22:4; 24:14, 22) and looked on itself as the messianic sect of Judaism.
Once we get into the intricacies of its teaching, we will be mesmer-
ized by its value to the church and the life of the church.

AUTHOR

OPTIONS FOR AUTHORSHIP

We must begin with the fact that James claims to be written by
"James, a servant of God and of the Lord Jesus Christ" (1:1). James
(Hebrew *Ya'aqov*; Greek *Iakōbos*) was a common name, and there
are four mentioned in the New Testament:

1. James the brother of John and son of Zebedee, disciples of
   Jesus (Mark 1:19; 3:17; Luke 6:14; Acts 1:13).
2. James the son of Alphaeus and also one of the Twelve (Mark
   3:18; 15:40; Matt 10:3; Luke 6:15; Acts 1:13).
3. James the father of Judas (Luke 6:16; Acts 1:13).
4. James the brother of Jesus and head elder of the Jerusalem
   church (Mark 6:3; Matt 13:55; Acts 15:13).
5. The final option is that it is a pseudonymous (falsely
   ascribed) letter written under the name of Jesus' brother,
   but penned by an unknown author.

---

2. All of the General Letters were questioned at one time or the other for
this reason.

It is generally agreed that the second and third options are too obscure (they do not take part by name in any of the action in the Gospels or Acts). Pseudonymity is a popular view among critical scholars, who believe it is very unlikely that a letter with such literary sophistication could have been written by a Jew who was the son of a carpenter (if the Lord's brother) or the son of a fisherman (if John's brother). The **Hellenistic** figures of speech ("course of ... life," 3:6) and literary flow are, it is argued, too far above a Galilean peasant.

However, this line of argument has been overturned in recent years as studies have shown the widespread use of Greek in Palestine and the high quality of many writings. Especially in Galilee the knowledge of Greek was at a high level, and for a Galilean Jew to have written James is no longer seen as far-fetched. Greek would have been spoken by Jesus' family from the start as a second language, since Galilee had a large Hellenistic population. Throughout history, many great authors have come from impoverished families, and there is no reason why that could not have been the case with James. It would have been similar to Europeans in our time who normally speak three or four languages. If James is written to **diasporic** Jews living in Syria and Asia Minor (which is likely), this is even more the case. The language fits a highly literate Hellenistic Jewish writing of the first century. It does not have the highest quality of the sophists and other rhetoricians of that day, but is still excellent Greek.

Critical scholars also doubt authorship by Jesus' or John's brothers because of the paucity of references to Jesus Christ (only Jas 1:1; 2:1). However, there are many implicit citations to the *Logia Jesu* (sayings of Jesus), with some scholars thinking as many as fifty or sixty explicit and implicit allusions are found in James. So while Jesus is not explicitly named often in this letter, it is steeped in his thought world and draws from him at virtually every juncture.

That leaves two options to choose from: the brother of John and one of the inner circle of the Twelve (with Simon Peter and

John); or the brother of Jesus, chief elder of the Jerusalem churches. The problem with the first is that he was martyred by Herod quite early, about AD 43-44 (see Acts 12), just a bit too early for the writing of this letter. Moreover, James the brother of Jesus has been the person associated with this letter from the very start and fits perfectly.

JAMES THE LORD'S BROTHER IN THE NEW TESTAMENT

There were five brothers and a few sisters of Jesus (Mark 6:3), and all were unbelievers (John 7:3-5) until Jesus appeared to them after his resurrection from the dead (1 Cor 15:7). They quickly joined the apostles and 120 in Jerusalem awaiting the Spirit's arrival at Pentecost (Acts 1:13-14). Most likely all his brothers and sisters became active in the new movement, but two in particular, Jude and James, became authors of a New Testament letter.

I would guess that James always regretted that he never knew Jesus on earth as a believer. However, he certainly made up for it quickly, becoming an elder in the Jerusalem church from the start. Galatians 1:18-19 tells how on Paul's first visit to Jerusalem after his conversion and ministry in Arabia, he met only with Cephas (Peter) and James, so this means James was already one of the leaders of the early church, named as one of the "apostles" in this passage. When Paul returned fourteen years later (most likely the "famine visit" of Acts 11:27-30), the three "pillars" were "James, Cephas, and John" (in that order, Gal 2:9). The fact that he is named first of the three demonstrates that he was accepted as leader of the Jerusalem church at that time. This is corroborated in the fact that in Acts 15:13 James addressed the Jerusalem Council virtually as the leader of the Jerusalem church, and in 21:18-19 Paul gives his report on the third missionary journey to "James, and all [the rest of] the elders."

Some see a growing conflict between James and Paul when Paul mentions that "certain men came from James" (Gal 2:12), saying that James himself may have led opposition to Paul in Acts 15 and

Galatians 1:7; 6:13. Yet there is no evidence of this in Galatians 2:12. These men were most likely representatives of the Jerusalem church sent to Galatia to encourage obedience to the Jerusalem letter of Acts 15:22–29. They were not opponents of Paul but still led Peter to cease eating with Gentiles (Gal 2:11–13). Paul rightfully had to castigate Peter for this hypocrisy, but conflict between James and Paul never truly materialized.

James was known even by fellow Jews as one of the most pious observers of Torah in all the land. (He was known as "James the Just.") When he was martyred in AD 62, the Jewish historian Josephus called it one of the atrocities that led to the rebellion of AD 66–70.[3] Some have listed him as one of the **Judaizers** who demanded that Christians live as Jews in obedience to Torah, but that is untrue. He was a faithful observer of the law like Paul himself, but as a Christian, not a Jew, and he was not a member of the "circumcision party" in the church. He and Paul had much the same theological perspective, but James stayed within the Jewish Christian world while Paul spearheaded the Gentile movement.

PROVENANCE AND DATE

Those who accept James as a pseudonymous letter tend to date its writing quite late, many at the turn of the first century, and the Tübingen school of F. C. Baur (1830s) at AD 150. Those who agree with me that James the Lord's brother wrote this letter sometimes place it as late as AD 61–62, just before his untimely demise, but it is better to see it as written in the mid-40s because there is no mention of the later Paul and the Gentile mission of the church. If this early date is correct, James is the first New Testament writing and blazed a very important trail in early church history.

A popular view sees James responding to a perversion of Paul's early teaching. This is a viable theory, but the issues of justification or of Abraham and faith and works could easily have preceded

---

3. Josephus, *Antiquities* 20.197–203.

Paul. James could well be discussing them because they are critical issues in the Jewish-Christian churches, not because of misunderstandings of Paul. Thus I conclude that James is writing before the debate between Paul and the Judaizers erupted, and he is developing his own theology of the relation between the Mosaic law and Christian freedom and grace in Christ. He and Paul are saying much the same thing, as we will see in the commentary proper.

The Jewish-Christian recipients of this letter experienced a great deal of oppression and persecution at the hands of ungodly rich landowners (Jas 2:6-7; 5:1-6). They were also discriminated against by fellow believers (2:1-6) and were often impoverished, lacking sufficient food and clothes (2:15-16). The pressures on them led to discouragement but also to dissension and backbiting as they took out their frustrations on each other. They became "double-minded," wavering between obeying God and centering on their earthly concerns (1:8; 4:8). James penned these words to provide an antidote for the spiritual sickness that had overtaken them.

He calls his readers "the twelve tribes," Jewish Christians scattered abroad outside Palestine, most likely in Syria and Asia Minor (1:1). This closely fits the rest of the letter, as in the use of the term "synagogue" for the church (2:2; NIV: "meeting") and the **midrashic** use of the Old Testament throughout. If we take "diaspora" in 1:1 literally as a reference to the Jewish believers "scattered" outside Palestine (as I do), these would be the congregations outside Israel, perhaps in Phoenicia, Cyprus, and Antioch as noted in Acts 11:19.

However, there is widespread disagreement over the situation of the recipients. Some say they were enduring the social upheaval under the Zealots in Galilee in the early 60s, and others the social upheavals in general in the 50s and 60s. However, there is no hint of rebellions or Zealot activity, and seeing the letter as addressing the ethical issues faced during the period of the Jewish-Christian church in the 40s seems a much better option. So this is a pastoral letter to diasporic communities addressing ethical sins and church dissension.

CANONICITY

None of the New Testament authors were aware that they were producing works that would join Genesis, Proverbs, or Isaiah as canonical writings of the church. However, once there was a growing realization of God's intentions in inspiring these writings, there was constant discussion of which works belonged in the list. Some were almost automatically placed on the list (the Gospels, the chief letters of Paul), but the General, or Catholic, Letters (James, 1–2 Peter, 1–3 John, and Jude) provoked extensive debate, and few writings experienced the peaks and valleys that James did on its way to being included in the canon.

Marcion and the **gnostics** rejected it in the mid-second century because of its Jewish character, and it is missing from the Muratorian Canon (around AD 200). There are several allusions to it in other early writings (for instance, in 1 Clement; 2 Clement 6:3–4; and Shepherd of Hermas—all late first to early second century), but there is an absence of direct recognition of it as Scripture until Origen in the third century. The church historian Eusebius in the fourth century still placed it among the "disputed books" (*Ecclesiastical History* 3.25.3). By that time, James was largely accepted in the Eastern church and by Athanasius, Jerome, and Cyril in the Western church, but it was not as well known there. It had become more popular by medieval times, and the English monk Venerable Bede wrote a commentary on it in the eighth century.

During the Reformation, the letter of James fell on hard times. Luther called it "an epistle of straw" because of the absence of strong teaching on Christ, and it was often regarded as secondary compared to the Gospels and Paul. This was not the case everywhere (Ulrich Zwingli and Philipp Melanchthon used it extensively), but it tended to be neglected. Today it has made a comeback in popularity, with many appreciating it greatly for its practical relevance and the quality of its teaching.

GENRE AND LITERARY STYLE

James has been identified variously as a letter, a wisdom writing, and a homily. Likely it is a combination of all three, for no single genre seems to suffice. For a letter, there are few personal touches, and it has always been seen as a "general letter" because it is not associated with a specific set of churches. The wisdom tone is very apparent, but few would wish to label it a wisdom writing on the level of Proverbs; the wisdom themes for the most part are derived from Jesus and his teaching. And finally, while it contains the paraenesis or exhortation of a homily, it should not be identified as only a homily. It could be identified as a set of synagogue homilies using wisdom material, but it is not a loose collection, for as we will see under "structure" below, it is a coherent, carefully controlled organizational whole, not an artificial collection.

With regard to style, James foregoes the normal introductory niceties—the greeting, thanksgiving, and opening prayer—and gets right to the critical issues his audience is facing. Apart from frequent uses of "brothers and sisters" (Jas 1:2, 16, 19; 2:1, 5, 14; 3:1, 10, 12; 4:11; 5:7, 9, 10, 12, 19), there are few personal touches in the letter. This could cause us to label it a treatise rather than a personal letter, but even though James had seemingly not met most of the people he was writing to, there is still a strong pastoral tone. The shape this pastoral tone takes is not so much to encourage beleaguered believers as to exhort and challenge weak Christians who are not really living faithfully according to their calling. There is a higher percentage of imperatives here than in any other New Testament writing; every section relates to the ethical imperative to live a life pleasing to God.

STRUCTURE AND OUTLINE

There are four different kinds of structure that have been proposed for this letter:

1. Martin Dibelius[4] was very influential with his view that James is a loose collection of isolated ethical meditations along the lines of rabbinic pearl-stringing or proverbs. These thematic studies are linked by catchwords that bring together the various units and move the thought along from one idea to the next. In recent decades, however, the ideas have been seen as more of a unified outline.

2. A topical approach sees the key themes of the letter being formed together in a unified ethical exhortation. Each section develops a theme, like trials (1:3–18), proper conduct (1:19–27), discrimination (2:1–13), faith without works (2:14–26), the tongue (3:1–12), wisdom (3:13–18), conflict (4:1–12), wealth (4:13–5:6), and patience (5:7–11). This is the approach taken by most today.

3. Others see macro- and micro-approaches to the topics of the book, with major themes controlling the structure and subthemes used to develop the message, followed by a conclusion at the end. Peter Davids as well as Craig Blomberg and Mariam Kamell, for instance, find three such macro-themes—testing/trials, wisdom, and poverty/wealth—introducing the three in 1:2–11; restating them in 1:12–27 (vv. 12–18 [trials], 19–26 [wisdom], 27 [poverty]); and finally expanding each in 2:1–5:18 (2:1–26 [riches/poverty]; 3:1–4:12 [wisdom and the tongue]; 4:13–5:18 [trials]).

4. It has also become popular to use discourse analysis and view the letter through the lens of Hellenistic rhetoric, since many Jews like Paul and perhaps even James were trained to some extent in these patterns of thought. After a lengthy introduction (1:2–27) and body opening (2:1–11), and before the body closing (4:13–5:6) and conclusion

---

4. For publication information for this and the others mentioned in this section, see the bibliography on page 177.

(5:7–20), many of these scholars see an elaborate **chiasm** like the following:

A 2:1–26
   B 3:1–12
      C 3:13–18
   B′ 4:1–3
A′ 4:4–10

The difficulty with this option is the incredible complexity of this rhetorical outline. There are way too many layers to be believable.

In finding the structure for this commentary, I began with noting the obvious sections and the fact that they are easily discernible because each centers on a particular theme (the second approach above). Then I organized the themes on the basis of how they relate to one another and outline the developing thought of James. His is a series of ethical meditations developing a wisdom writing that tells his readers how to live life according to God's will and how to conduct themselves so as to please and obey God at all times.

After teaching James for many years and working seriously on the structure of his thought, I have come to the conclusion that he, like Matthew, organizes his logical flow into a series of triads. Those who think James is a loosely organized collection of isolated homilies (option one above) have not adequately considered the literary cohesiveness and carefully constructed coherence of this letter. It is in reality woven together very tightly, and I enjoy anew every time I am privileged to teach or write on his magnificent work.

Greeting (1:1)
I. The testing of your faith (1:2–18)
   A. Trials and testing (1:2–11)
      1. Joy in the midst of trials (1:2–4)
      2. Wisdom and faith in trials (1:5–8)
         a. The need to pray for wisdom (1:5)

THEOLOGY OF THE LETTER

As mentioned above, Luther and others have disparaged James largely because they find him weak theologically, thinking he is so concerned with the practical things of the Christian life that he has ignored theological depth. Especially when compared to Paul, he seems to have little on Christology, **soteriology**, the Holy Spirit, or the mission of the church to the world. The truth is that James is one of the shorter letters (108 verses total), and like all letters it is occasional, discussing only those issues that were problematic at that time among the audience. So it says little regarding matters that were settled, and there is no systematic presentation of dogma. However, this doesn't mean it is theologically shallow. Indeed, it is a very theological work, focused on the Christian walk and faithful obedience to God's demands. The dichotomy between theology and the practical side of wisdom and the Christian walk is a false one; practical issues like trials of the faith, discrimination, and the tongue are theological at their core.

GOD

The most frequently mentioned reality in this letter is God, stressed sixteen times: "Father" appears three times (1:17, 27; 3:9) and "Lord" seven times (1:7; 3:9; 4:10, 15; 5:4, 10, 11). Jesus is "Lord" in 1:1; 2:1; 5:7, 8. Prayer "in the name of the Lord" (5:14–15) could refer to either one. God is the archetypal model for the conduct of his people. Their biggest problem is duplicity, being double-minded rather than focused on God (1:8; 4:8), and God in his oneness provides the antidote for that spiritual illness (2:19). The ever-shifting, unstable world of the shallow Christian can only be turned around by the God of creation, the "Father of the heavenly lights" (1:17) who brings stability and wholeness into our lives.

Israel is the bride of Yahweh and the church the bride of Christ, so it is only natural that when his bride strays and commits adultery, God is jealous and angry for her perfidy (4:5). When his people seek "friendship with the world," they become enemies of God (4:4) and fall under his judgment. However, he is also loving and compassionate, giving his unfaithful people "more grace" to repent and find forgiveness (4:6). Out of divine love, he wants his bride back and faithful to him.

As a gracious Lord, he pours into our lives "every good and perfect gift" (1:17), even the "crown of life" (1:12). However, it is mandatory that we in turn open ourselves up and submit, repenting and drawing near to him in submission (4:7–10). As the Lawgiver and Judge (4:12), he demands that we who have received his mercy show that mercy to those around us (2:13).

TRIALS, TESTS, AND TEMPTATIONS

James chooses trials as his opening theme, and it permeates his letter. The Greek term is *peirasmos*, which actually has three connotations depending on the context. Put together, it refers to a trial or area of difficulty in life that, when sent from God, becomes a test of our faith. At the same time, it awakens self and the flesh, becoming a temptation to sin. Several of the areas I will be discussing below, in fact, are trials, such as poverty, illness, or the effects of backbiting. At the outset, James defines trials as tests of faith and notes that they have "many kinds" (1:2–3). God's purpose in allowing them is to test our commitment to him and the degree of our separation from the world, thereby enabling us to learn perseverance and become "mature and complete" spiritually (1:4). In a real sense, this is the motto of the letter.

There are three types of suffering in the letter: external persecution from enemies of the gospel, especially wealthy landowners who oppose poor believers (2:6–7; 5:1–6); personal suffering through poverty and illness (1:9–10; 5:13–18); and internal mistreatment by other believers through discrimination and backbiting (2:1–13; 4:1–10). In all of these, God's people must depend on him to vindicate them and overturn the harmful deeds done against them.

In each area of suffering, the trials become temptation as we are drawn away from God to self, resulting first in sin and then in spiritual death (1:15). There are two sources of this temptation: first, what the Jewish people labeled the "evil *yetzer*," or impulse, the fleshly side of temptation. This tendency to self-centered living permeates every section of this letter—the "filth and the evil" of 1:21, the favoritism of 2:1, the self-deception of 2:16, the fiery tongue of 3:6, the battles of the tongue in 4:1, and the selfish ambition of 4:16. Second, temptation often originates in Satan, the external source who sets the whole being on fire (3:6, 15).

ESCHATOLOGY

James is not just a wisdom-dispensing prophet demanding ethical accountability in this world; he is also an **apocalyptic** seer who places all his ethical exhortations in the context of final **eschatology**—that is, the last days, when this world will come to an end and eternity will be ushered in. This perspective begins in 1:9–11, where the earthly environment of rich and poor (= exaltation and humiliation) are reversed. The "crown of life" awaits the faithful poor, who receive this victory through perseverance (1:12).

This will take place at the **eschaton**, the end of the age; for sinners it will end in death (1:15), in contrast to the inheritance awaiting the poor (2:5). The divine Judge of 2:12–13 and 4:12 will sit on his *bēma* (judgment seat) at the last judgment and give the "greater condemnation" (3:1 KJV); that is, those who fail in their commitment to him "will be judged more strictly."

The ungodly rich of 5:1–6 prosper in this life at the expense of the poor but have a terrifying future awaiting them in which they will answer for their sins. They have turned themselves into the fattened cows headed for the slaughter at the last judgment (5:5), in contrast to the faithful poor, who must have patience as they await their final vindication on that same day (5:7).

James has a perfect balance between the already and the not-yet. The present is the time of patient perseverance in light of the divine promises that the wealthy oppressors will receive their just due. This is not a totally apocalyptic work with a focus entirely on the future, for it is also a wisdom writing with a present focus centering on our righteousness and walk with Christ. James's is an "inaugurated eschatology," with present righteous living preparing for future reward.

WEALTH AND POVERTY

It would be excessive to call wealth and poverty the central issue of the book; ethical faithfulness to God in general is central. Still, it is very important and appears in every chapter. James begins in 1:9–11 by extolling God's humbling of the wealthy and exaltation of the poor. As in the Old Testament, God has a special place for the marginalized and needy of this world (Deut 10:18–19; Ps 68:5) and wants his people to lift them up and care for them in their time of suffering (Jas 1:27). The sin of discrimination against the poor (2:1–13) was especially onerous and under indictment from God. In 2:6–7 we learn that discrimination against the poor was taken so far as even to favor wealthy enemies of the church when they visited the Christian synagogue; this was a serious sin.

The theme of wealth and poverty comes to full fruition in 4:13–5:11. It is critical to realize that James never says wealth is inherently evil. For James, wealth is a gift God bestows on people not so they can live luxuriously and lord it over others but so they can share their largesse with the needy and raise them up. Nevertheless, it can become a temptation to do evil, as in 4:13–17, where rich Christians are tempted to leave God out of their plans and take control of their own lives. Instead of living in humility under God (1:10), they demonstrate a worldly dependence on their wealth. In 5:1–6, the ungodly commit even worse sins, using their wealth to steal from their day laborers to feed their own appetites. Divine judgment will be the only wage they receive.

WISDOM, PRAYER, AND PRACTICAL CHRISTIANITY

The basic definition of biblical wisdom is "living life in God's world by God's rules." It has two foci—it deals with every area of life and it centers on dependence on God. James demands that we use the wisdom God has given us to live well in the practical areas of life. Wisdom is closely connected with prayer, beginning with 1:5–8. The truth is that we need wisdom from God since (Greek: *ei*) we lack wisdom, and we will receive it only through prayer (1:5b, "ask God, who gives generously"). The definition of wisdom with relation to life's needs and proper behavior is simple—to say, "If it is the Lord's will, we will live and do this or that" (4:15). Wisdom is seeking the Lord's will in everything we do.

The "good and perfect gift" that God gives us (1:17) is wisdom, and the result is "deeds done in the humility that comes from wisdom" (3:13). We ought to eschew false, so-called earthly wisdom and exhibit the "wisdom that comes from heaven," typified by purity and peace-loving action (3:15, 17). For James, wisdom is closely connected with conduct, and all of this letter is dedicated to developing the contours of wisdom in the practical areas of life. The divided mind of 1:6–8 is the antithesis of this proper behavior. Wisdom is exceedingly practical, dealing with the way we live as God's people and the relationships we maintain with others in the community.

The answer to maintaining this wise lifestyle is prayer, developed in three passages. First, in 1:5 the wisdom to make God-pleasing choices comes as a gift from God when we pray (see also 1:17; 3:17). We cannot achieve this on our own, but our generous God supplies the wisdom we need. Second, we must exhibit radical surrender and place all our needs before him in prayer. This is stated negatively in 4:2-3: "You do not have because you do not ask God." The simple truth is that we must relinquish control of our lives to him, as in 4:13-16. Third, this type of God-dependent prayer is exemplified with respect to illness in 5:13-18, where "the prayer of a righteous person is powerful and effective," both physically and spiritually.

SPEECH, THE OUTWARD SIGN OF THE SOUL

The misuse of the tongue for selfish purposes—to gain power over others and to slander those you want to hurt—was a major problem in James's churches. The issue is introduced in what some would call the theme verse of the letter: "Everyone should be quick to listen, slow to speak and slow to become angry" (1:19). When anger is directing a loose tongue, serious trouble is in store. These three areas surface again in the central section, 3:1-4:12, where envy and selfish ambition produce backbiting and angry retorts rather than a wise use of the tongue to build up the church. The ABA pattern centers on wisdom's providing the antidote, bringing peace and "a harvest of righteousness" (3:13-18) to overcome dissension in the community (3:1-12; 4:1-12). For James, people's speech habits show the true state of their spiritual walk with God. The phrase "quick to listen" in 1:19 refers primarily to listening to God, and entails obedience to his commands. The "humility" of 3:13 will result in the submission of 4:7-8, as God takes over and leads us to victory over self and sin.

LAW AND GRACE

As I have argued above (see "Provenance and Date"), James is writing before the Judaizers developed their heretical views and before Paul developed his law-versus-grace theology in opposition to them. The Torah is highlighted in three places in James— 1:25 ("the perfect law that gives freedom"); 2:8–12 ("the royal law found in Scripture … the law that gives freedom"); and 4:11–12 ("There is only one Lawgiver and Judge, the one who is able to save and destroy").

There are several things we must conclude from these observations: (1) James is completely positive about the law. (2) He always sees the law in terms of its ethical mandates, not its cultic requirements; he never demands adherence to the cultic rituals, but at the same time he never negates them either. (3) The law seems to be completely accepted by his churches; he uses it to support his arguments and needs no arguments for its validity. (4) James is Christian before he is Jewish; there is no hint that salvation is found in anything other than faith in Christ. (5) He is very Jewish regarding the law; it is the "perfect law that gives freedom" (1:25). He does not show the negativity toward the law that led Paul to say that it was "our guardian until Christ came" (Gal 3:24) and that we have "died to the law" (Rom 7:4). As a result, some scholars think that James is antithetical to Paul on the law, that Paul considers the law an enslaving force while James thinks it a liberating force.

On the surface, that seems viable. But we have to remember that Paul expressed a negative attitude about the law only when opposing the Judaizers, for whom the law became a means of legalistic salvation. By contrast, in Romans 7:12 Paul said "the law is holy, and the commandment is holy, righteous and good." Moreover, James is in agreement with Jesus in Matthew 5:18: "Truly I tell you, until heaven and earth disappear, not the smallest letter, not the least stroke of a pen, will by any means disappear from the Law." There is no contradiction between the two. Paul stresses one aspect of the place of the law in the age of Christ, James another. Paul emphasizes the legal aspect, the place of the law in the new salvation inaugurated in Christ. For James, the law is a guide to moral living, pleasing God in one's conduct.

I have often said that if you can't preach James you simply can't preach—period. It virtually preaches itself. Only Proverbs can match this letter for its practicality. It touches on nearly all the issues of life and is pure joy to study. So if I can't help you enjoy a deep Bible study on James, I doubt I can make you enjoy anything! Read these wondrous thoughts (not mine but those of James himself) and prepare to be touched to the core of your being.

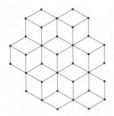

TESTING AND TEMPTATION
(1:1–18)

James is in many ways the most practical book in the Bible. This first section (1:1–18) introduces the three key issues of this letter—the need to endure trials as a test intended by God to strengthen us (vv. 2–4, 12–15), the need for wisdom and dependence on God to be victorious in the test (vv. 5–8), the problem of poverty-stricken Christians (vv. 9–11), and God's perfect gift—life (vv. 16–18). The rest of the letter will build on these themes.

The traditional practice in ancient letters was to open with a greeting, followed by a section detailing thanksgiving and prayer. James, because of the seriousness of the issues and his concern for these churches, skips these elements and gets right to addressing problems. The basic trial is poverty, and the only way to triumph over this test of faith is a deep trust in God and the wisdom to overcome temptations. James begins here because all the other situations he will address—prejudice, putting faith to work, the danger of the tongue, and oppression by the wealthy—flow out of this central trial.

JAMES GREETS HIS AUDIENCE (1:1)

Ancient letters, and most of those in the New Testament, normally opened with the author identifying himself and then greeting the

recipient by name. James begins by calling himself "a servant of
God and of the Lord Jesus Christ." Immediately two issues arise.
First, the Greek *doulos* should be translated "slave" rather than
"servant." James, like most of the authors of New Testament letters (Paul in numerous places, Peter in 2 Pet 1:1), is proud of the
privilege of serving God and Christ with absolute allegiance. As
in the Old Testament, he is "God's special possession" (1 Pet 2:9).
It is meaningful that he does not label himself Jesus' brother or
even an apostle (as Paul does in Gal 1:19). He centers on the deeper
reality, in keeping with biblical precedent, as Old Testament leaders called themselves slaves of Yahweh (Deut 34:5; Jer 33:21; Ezek
37:25). In the ancient world, slaves often wielded the authority of
their masters and were considered part of their family.

Second, many have thought "God" here is not God the Father
but Jesus himself. If so, this would be translated, "slave of Jesus
Christ, who is God and Lord." This is possible and would resemble John 1:1, 18, where *theos* refers to the deity of Christ. In 2 Peter
1:1, where this is the case, it reads "the righteousness of our God
and Savior Jesus Christ," because the Greek indicates this.[1] That
is not the case here, and it is best to read them as two separate
members of the Godhead with the NIV, "a servant of God and of
the Lord Jesus Christ." They are equally the masters over James,
but it is Father and Son, not Jesus alone.

The recipients are "the twelve tribes scattered among the
nations." This is highly unusual and seems to describe the
diasporic Jews living outside Palestine. It could be literal,
describing Jewish Christians outside the borders of the Holy
Land, or it could be metaphorical for the church as the "new
Israel," rejected by both Jew and Gentile and thus the "scattered

---

1. It follows what is called "Sharp's rule," named after Granville Sharp, who
proposed it in 1798. According to Sharp's rule, when a single Greek article
appears before the first of two nouns, it brings the two together into a con-
ceptual unity.

ones" living in Gentile lands. It probably is both: the Jewish-Christian churches of Asia Minor as the righteous remnant gathered by God from the twelve tribes, reestablished as his people with the twelve apostles over them and (together with Gentile Christians) constituting the new and true Israel of the new covenant age. In them the promised restoration of Israel spoken of in Isaiah 11:1–2 and Ezekiel 37:21–22 has taken place, and God's people are together in Christ.

HAVE JOY IN THE MIDST OF TRIALS (1:2–4)

James addresses this to his "brothers and sisters" because they are all part of the family of God. The church is an assembly of people meeting together, but is much more a family sharing and caring for each other. I have often called James 1:2 the "impossible command": "consider it pure joy, my brothers and sisters, whenever you face trials of many kinds." Am I supposed to pray, "Thank you, Lord, that these things have gone so wrong for me; by the way, could I have some further trials so I can have even more joy"? The verb "consider" means to "think, regard" and speaks of mental effort to regard an event from a certain vantage point, in this case from God's perspective. Hebrews 12:11 gives us the other side of this: "No discipline seems pleasant at the time, but painful." Considered from the human perspective, there is little but hurt and pain to be gained from our earthly travails. Looking at it from God's side, James is emphatic. These very same difficulties are in reality "pure joy" (*pasan charan*) not because of what we are going through but because of who is in charge of our lives.

The key to understanding this is to separate joy from happiness. We are happy when everything is going smoothly and for our benefit. True joy only comes when we realize God is behind a trial and working it out for our good (Rom 8:28). When we surrender to his providential care, we have peace and find joy. "Fall into" (*peripesēte*; NIV: "face") pictures a person walking on a smooth path suddenly tumbling into a black hole. Moreover, these trials do not conveniently come one at a time but "many kinds" of them hit us at odd times from odd angles when we are not ready for them.

The term "trial" (*peirasmos*) is used two different ways in this chapter. It is both a "test" that God sends to strengthen us (see 1 Pet 1:6; 4:12) and a "temptation" that can trip us up spiritually (1 Pet 1:13–15). This also defines Jesus' "temptation narrative" recorded in Matthew 4 and Luke 4. From Satan's perspective he was *tempting* Jesus, but in reality he was a tool God was using to *test* his Son. Tests are essential to the spiritual growth of every one of us, and God tested all of his chosen leaders—Abraham at the sacrifice of Isaac (Gen 22), Moses on the mountain (Exod 34:28), Israel in the wilderness (Num 14:33–34), and Elijah in the wilderness (1 Kgs 19:8). In this letter, the primary trials are poverty and persecution, but by saying "many kinds," James wants to include all the vicissitudes of life that so discourage us. Still, the external test of persecution and the resultant poverty of those who have lost everything are uppermost.

Verse 2 tells *how* we should react to trials; verse 3 tells *why* we should react that way. When we think carefully about our situation and where the Lord is in all this, we "know that the testing of [our] faith produces endurance." This is introduced by a causal participle (*ginōskontes*, "because you know") that often introduces catechetical material: important theological truths the early church recognized and wanted to preserve for future generations. This explains the purpose of trials: they are tests sent by God to teach us to persevere by trusting entirely in him. "Testing" is *dokimion*, a term that has two aspects: first, the refining process that makes a metal (or person) pure; and second, the results of the test—namely, the genuineness or approval of the person or thing when the process is finished. Here the emphasis is on the means by which we are tested, while in the parallel 1 Peter 1:7 the stress is on the results: "the proven genuineness of your faith—of greater worth than gold."

God allows (and even sends) trials because they test our faith and refine our spiritual walk. The refiner's fire then strengthens our faith by teaching us to persevere. Like gold, our faith must be tested in the crucible of life so that it can be purified and become genuine, resulting in our approval by God. The fires of trials bring out the impurities so that God, the cosmic goldsmith, can remove them and make us "pure gold" spiritually.

"Perseverance" (or "endurance") is not a weak or passive waiting for God to act but refers to an active patience that gets to work in our lives for God. This patient, active faith is produced (*katergazomai*) in us, an agricultural metaphor describing the process of growth producing a harvest in our lives. The verbs here are present tense, picturing continual growth. In other words, we are enabled by our trials to wait on the Lord more and more effectively over time.

The idea that suffering producing endurance was common in Jewish thought and literature.[2] Two other New Testament passages develop this idea (Rom 5:3-5 and 1 Pet 1:6-7). They all get at the same basic truth—God sends trials to strengthen our level of surrender and trust in him. He does so because earthly difficulties force us to trust him rather than ourselves or the world we inhabit, with the result that we learn how to patiently wait on him and so become spiritually pure, gaining his approval.

James 1:4 tells us what we must do to put this to work in our lives: "Let perseverance finish its work so that you may be mature and complete, not lacking anything." The idea of letting it "finish its work" refers to producing its "full or complete end." In other words, God sends the refining process, the trials that become a divine test intended to purify us and enable us to grow and mature. We are then responsible to permit trials to complete their task by allowing them to work in our lives. We are the farmers who must

---

2. See Jubilees 2:7; Testament of Joseph 2:7; 10:11.

let it grow and produce its God-intended crop. "Finish its work" is literally "continue to have its full or perfect effect." It often will take a long time to finish this process, to both yield to God and to allow the effects to take place.

"Mature" (*teleioi*) can also be translated "perfect," indicating the situation when the process is completed and believers experience God's perfect purpose in their lives. It is a dynamic, active process that takes great effort. The persevering Christian then becomes "complete" or "whole." The two Greek terms are near synonyms, both connoting God's complete, perfect work in us. Believers become all God intends them to be, whole people and fully mature. The second is a medical metaphor, referring to a "sound" or "whole" body, completely healthy in every area. In other words, as believers learn to persevere in difficult situations, they begin to become mature followers and attain spiritual wholeness.

The goal here is the same as Matthew 5:48: "Be perfect, therefore, as your heavenly Father is perfect." Of course, perfection will not fully arrive until we have entered our heavenly existence, but we are to strive for it and seek to grow at all times. This becomes a major theme, stressed also in James 1:17, 25; 3:2, and means we surrender to God's divine work in us and seek to allow his work to produce a new character in us, a foretaste of heaven.

As they grow in Christ, well-rounded Christians discover they are "not lacking anything." They have no needs, for God has supplied everything, and Christ has fulfilled all their wants. This truth is stated perfectly in Philippians 4:19: "And my God will meet all your needs according to the riches of his glory in Christ Jesus." The trials of our faith are a spiritual necessity in that they test our Christian character and teach us spiritual endurance, thereby making us complete in Christ and perfectly whole or healthy spiritually. We have all our needs met by God and thus find perfect contentment (see also Phil 4:11–13).

SHOW WISDOM AND FAITH IN TRIALS (1:5-8)

In 1:2-4 James developed the problem of trials and the need to overcome them (the what and the why), and now in verses 5-8 he discusses the "how"—that is, the solution for overcoming them: namely, through wisdom and faith.[3] This flows naturally from verse 4, where those who allow endurance to do its perfect work in them lack nothing. Here James turns to the one thing all too many of us do lack: wisdom to encounter our trials successfully.

THE NEED TO PRAY FOR WISDOM (1:5)

Here James employs what is called "a condition of fact" (Greek: *ei*, "if"), assuming the truthful reality of the problem. The beginning could be translated, "Since you of course lack the wisdom you need. ..." Wisdom (Greek: *sophia*) is an essential trait we must possess if we are to overcome our difficulties and grow to spiritual maturity and wholeness. In the Old Testament it was seen as an attribute of God (Dan 2:20-23) given to chosen leaders like Solomon (1 Kgs 10:23-24) and made available to those who fear God (Prov 1:7; 9:10; 15:33).

Wisdom is one of the core motifs in James. It is a practical use of knowledge in our lives, but it is also much more. As in the Old Testament Wisdom literature, it is more about our reliance on the presence of God in our lives. It refers to living life in God's world according to God's rules, embracing both a practical orientation (including every area of life and conduct) and a dependence on God (reverence and submission to his commands). It is divine, not human, wisdom that we need, and that is exactly what

---

3. Some believe this is the first of many places where unrelated material is artificially placed together, and that the only connection between verses 2-4 and 5-8 is the catchword "lack." However, I strongly disagree and join the many who see the two sections as a closely related unity (as the discussion will demonstrate).

is promised in Proverbs 2:6: "The LORD gives wisdom." This is possible only when the people of God keep his commands in their hearts (Prov 3:1). Only a spiritual ability to recall and follow God's truths will suffice.

Wisdom is inherently practical, which means God guides us in the needs of practical everyday life. It is not the obverse of the spiritual realm but rather details the arena in which the spiritual life works itself out. Jesus was a teacher of wisdom (Matt 11:2–19, 25–30; 23:34–39), and Paul speaks of "the depth of the riches of the wisdom and knowledge of God" (Rom 11:33) as well as "the manifold wisdom of God" (Eph 3:10).

Since none of us have in ourselves the *sophia* we need, there is only one solution: "ask God." Wisdom is not a natural human ability and can only be attained when we realize it is a gift from God that we acquire only when we ask him for it. There is no seminary course in practical wisdom or set of seminars where we can be taught its principles. We can only receive it from a loving, giving Father as the result of sincere prayer. Yet he is a God who gives; the present tense means that it is an ongoing gift to us.

Two added points show how extensive this giving is. Wisdom is given "generously," and it is given "to all" who ask. The term *haplōs* can mean "singly" or "generously." The first would mean "singleness of heart" and refer to God's undivided intention to meet our needs. God gives to us without reservation, fully centered on caring for our every need. The second centers on his liberal nature, meaning that he gives way beyond all our expectations, more than we could ever imagine. I refuse to see an either-or here but believe the emphasis is on the richness of meaning. There is a definite contrast with the "double-minded person" of 1:6—God is single-minded and gives without hesitation or limit in his generosity. The ultimate foolishness is refusing to go to God and ask for the wisdom to handle all our trials and suffering.

The Greeks and Romans had only capricious gods who had little interest in the human plight and whose aid or involvement in people's lives had to be bought, usually by sacrifices and offerings. There is quite a different portrait of God in the Bible. There he is pictured as the covenant God who loves his people and makes them part of his family. He is constantly involved in meeting their needs, and when they wander off like sheep, he acts redemptively to bring them back. (Even his punishment is redemptive in the long run.) Matthew 7:7 says it well: "Ask and it will be given to you." We are responsible to bring our needs to the Lord, and he promises to respond. "Cast all your anxiety on him because he cares for you" (1 Pet 5:7).

God not only answers our prayers generously without any hesitation. He also does so "without finding fault" (*oneidizontos*), without mocking or reproaching us for our lack of wisdom. His purpose is to encourage the saints not to hesitate but to boldly go to him in prayer. He understands entirely our human weakness and will never make fun of us or belittle us for our failures. He does not give grudgingly or respond to our inadequacies with recrimination. Rather, he will give ("it will be given" is a divine passive, which indicates God as the giver) the needed wisdom to us. Note that this is not a "name it and claim it" prosperity theology. God is not promising us whatever we ask but rather will give us the wisdom to overcome when things go wrong. He is not promising health and wealth but instead the spiritual maturity to trust him to turn our disadvantages into spiritual growth.

The Need to Pray in Faith (1:6–8)

James next qualifies the promise and defines the conditions for proper prayer—namely, the critical importance of faith over doubting when coming to God in prayer (the word linking vv. 5 and 6 is "ask"). When we come to the Lord, we must "believe and not doubt." The Christian life is characterized by God-centeredness, as believers rely on him in every area of their life and exemplify that reliance in their prayer life, bringing everything before him for wisdom and guidance. When we ask in faith, we take him at his word and trust him implicitly, believing in his loving beneficence toward us. There is no certainty that he will grant our request but rather a certainty that he will hear us and do what is best for us. The faith referred to here is not saving faith but an active trust in God and in his constant care for us. We must remember that when God says "no" or "wait" to our requests it is because he loves us enough not to give us what we want. The old adage "Father knows best" is true in our prayer life.

We must define doubting very carefully. The term used is *diakrinomenos*, which does not mean what we normally think of as doubt—that is, to be uncertain whether God is going to grant our request. It stems from the idea of drawing distinctions between things, and here it is the mental act of having a "divided mind"—at one moment centered on God and at another centered on the world. Such a person is never settled spiritually but constantly wavering in commitment and trust in God. This kind of doubt is in regard to the kind of God we serve, whether we should trust him or ourselves. James is asking whether we truly believe he is our loving, giving Father, or whether we deep down consider him indifferent and thereby go our own way. This type of mindset involves not just doubting if God can or will do what he has been asked; it actually involves leaving God out of the situation and trying to meet the need by ourselves.

Because of this doubt, we can waver between God-centered and self-centered thinking. Such people, James says, resemble "a wave of the sea, blown and tossed by the wind." Their divided minds drive them back and forth and cause them to lose control spiritually. They become as unstable as the sea, not just during a typhoon but even in normal "weather," with the waves tossing us up and down and side to side. These ever-changing patterns of the sea become a perfect picture of what we sadly could call the normal Christian life with a worldly more than spiritual way of thinking. One moment we are trusting God; the next we are living for ourselves. We might call such people "spiritually seasick"—one minute up (centered on God), the next minute down (centered on the world).

There are two results to such a life—inner disquiet (v. 6b) and outward isolation from God (vv. 7–8). These up-and-down Christians "should not expect to receive anything from the Lord" since they are trusting him for very little. "Expect" is Greek *oiesthō*, "think, suppose," and so this could be translated "Don't imagine that you will receive anything." Since these people depend on blind luck as much as they do on God, they should never suppose God will reward them for their indecision by heeding their requests. God may give "good and perfect" gifts (1:17), but he gives these to those who are centered on him and ask him for them (4:2). Those who leave God out of their life much of the time should never expect much from him. They expect things to work out for them without recourse to God at work in their lives. However, he is not an overindulgent parent who keeps bailing out his narcissistic children from the messes they have got themselves into. If they want nothing from him, they will get nothing from him. As in James 4:2, "You do not have because you do not ask God."

The reason God will give them nothing is that they are "double-minded and unstable in all they do" (1:8). This phrase acts as a summary of verses 5–8. The doubter is a person who has multiple spiritual personalities and by definition is "unstable" in every area of her life. She is "double-minded" (*dipsychos*, only here and 4:8 in early Greek literature), and prayer must involve the whole mind if it is to be effective. Self-sufficiency negates prayer and forces God out of the situation. Again, this is so much more than what we normally think of as doubt, for it is a completely self-centered worldview with little room for God or dependence on him.

In short, James is referring to an uncaring failure to consider God and his place in one's life. It is not doubt understood as uncertainty but a deliberate and conscious refusal to trust God at any point—a faithless approach to life. This produces a restless person with no anchor or steady foundation to provide security for the future. The Greek behind "in all they do" is actually broader, "in all their ways" (*en pasais tais hodois autou*), referring to every area of life, not just actions. The complete instability caused by a divided mind and a self-centered lifestyle has destroyed any hope of peace or security in life.

JAMES EXPLORES THE SOCIAL DIMENSION:
POVERTY AND WEALTH (1:9–11)

There are three viable interpretations of this section: (1) It can refer to status, telling poor believers to glory in the fact that their social place in the Christian community is elevated in Christ, while wealthy believers should glory in their humiliation—that is, that in Christ they are lowered and made equal with others in the church. Both are equal before Christ, as the poor are made rich and the rich made poor. (2) Christians should be satisfied and do their duty wherever God places them, some made wealthy and others poor. Whatever the will of God is, glory in it. (3) The Christian poor should consider themselves fortunate (or elevated), for they are not tempted to worship mammon, while the non-Christian poor must come to grips with their problem with mammon, as it is resulting in their low status with God. As Christ said, "It is easier for a camel to go through the eye of a needle than for someone who is rich to enter the kingdom of God" (Mark 10:25).

One issue is the place of the wealthy in this letter. If the wealthy are portrayed in James as non-Christians, outside the community and enemies of the faithful, the third view is the correct one. While that is possible here, I do not think that is the case in the letter as a whole. James is not saying that all wealthy people are by nature opposed by God, nor is he saying here that Christians should be satisfied wherever God places them (option two). It is more likely that he is telling wealthy saints that they should take pride not in their high earthly status but in their humble spiritual status in Christ—in their dependence on Christ rather than their material possessions, and at the same time in their equality with the poor in the eyes of God. So the first is likely the best option.

This section connects to verses 2–8 by addressing one of the primary trials in the community: the trials suffered by the poor in the church. This is an unjust world that favors the rich over the poor, and we could ask where God is in all this injustice taking place around us. Is he an unjust judge who has accepted bribes to favor the wealthy? One of the goals of the early church was to create an environment that would ensure that "there were no needy persons among them" (Acts 4:32–34). James is telling the poor to learn to endure trials and warning the wealthy not to lord it over the poor. The church exists to elevate the lowly and humble the high and mighty. The result is that the poor can glory in the way God is going to raise them up, and the rich can glory in the way their earthly riches are going to perish.

THE EXALTATION OF THE LOWLY (1:9)

The rich don't undergo economic trials. They experience temptation, while it is the poor who pass through economic suffering and trials. The result is that these wealthy believers most often are the "double-minded" of verse 8, who all too easily ignore their need for God. Their wealth too easily removes any sense of need or commitment to God and leads to a total dependence on the things of the world. The social stratification that stood between rich and poor was even more pronounced in the Roman world than it is in our modern world. James emphasizes here that people are not superior just because they inherit wealth, but many of us act as if that is the case and deep down actually believe it is so. The teaching of all of Scripture is that before God all people are equal and must equally place their dependence on God rather than on their earthly resources. However, that is more easily said than done for the wealthy, who have so much of the world's resources at their disposal.

The point here is that the poor have a huge advantage in that their situation makes them depend on God. Thus they can open themselves more fully to him and find their joy in him. Of course, they can lust for a higher position in life and for more wealth, but their lack of possessions can mean they have much less pulling them back from God. "Believers in humble circumstances" are the poor, those who have little status in the world and are looked down on because of their poverty. In spite of all their difficulties, they have something in which they can "take pride," for the necessity of placing their trust entirely in God (they have few earthly goods) means he is more central in their lives. Therefore, they have a "high position" spiritually in him. "Take pride" is actually "boast" (*kauchasthō*), normally viewed as a sin (Rom 2:17, 23; 1 Cor 4:7; Eph 2:9), but Philippians 1:26 speaks of "boasting in Christ Jesus," and in Philippians 2:16 Paul says that he will "boast on the day of Christ." Pride in self is a sin, but pride in Christ (and others) is a privilege and joy. "High position" is actually "in their exaltation" (*en tō hypsei autou*), meaning in the fact that God has raised them high, far above their lowly status on earth.

There is a strong sense of inaugurated **eschatology** here, saying that they are now honored or exalted as citizens of heaven (Phil 3:20) and even now are inhabitants of heaven in a spiritual sense (Rev 12:2; 13:6) in spite of their alienation and deprivation in their earthly, pagan society. Their present glory will become absolute on the day Christ returns, when death is defeated once for all (1 Cor 15:55) and God's people enjoy their final eternal victory over evil. James is hardly saying that poverty is a good thing and that suffering is to be commended for its own sake. Rather, God uses even these sorrows for good (Rom 8:28), and these trials lead to spiritual growth. The exaltation begins now, but it is spiritual in the present and will be all-encompassing only in the future heavenly kingdom. Both God and the church are centered on the poor and elevating them in their difficult lives.

THE HUMILIATION OF THE WEALTHY (1:10–11)

The poor boast in the fact that Christ has exalted them above their earthly station. The boasting of the wealthy should rejoice in the opposite, that Christ will remove earthly glory and introduce justice. How can they rejoice in being humbled or brought low? They know that they are first believers and only secondarily are they rich, and so they are thrilled that evil is destroyed and the poor people of God exalted to their true and proper estate. No wealthy person wants to lose riches, but all should want to use their riches to alleviate the suffering of the poor. Their goal is not to glory in their superiority but to use their advantages to help others.

There are two aspects to this: (1) All earthly possessions are transitory and will cease to exist, a truth often stressed in the Old Testament (Job 3:14–15; 15:29–30; Pss 49:16–20; 73:12, 18–20). This basic principle is meant to set our sights on God rather than the things of this life. (2) The rich boast and rejoice in the fact that they equally, along with the poor, belong to God and Christ and can depend on them in every area of life, as expressed well in Jeremiah 9:23–24: "Let not ... the strong boast of their strength or the rich boast of their riches, but let the one who boasts boast about this: that they have the understanding to know me." All, rich and poor alike, stand equal in the church and belong to the same family.

All of this is grounded in the reality of the transitory nature of human life and earthly things. James uses vegetation as his example in 1:10–11, building on passages like Job 14:2; Psalm 103:5; and Isaiah 40:6–8. A "wild flower" is temporary, lasting just the spring and part of the summer, "for the sun rises with scorching heat and withers the plant; its blossom falls and its beauty is destroyed." Death rather than life governs this fallen world, and the only thing we can count on is that earthly things will pass. The picture is that of the sirocco, the hot wind coming off the desert in Palestine that can wither a beautiful flower literally in seconds. Life is transient, and death comes swiftly. One day the fields of Galilee are bursting with wildflowers and color, and the next they are brown, and it's all gone. The description is graphic—the scorching sun rises, the plant is withered, the blossoms fall off the stalk, and its beauty is gone.

As the rich "go about their business" and pursue wealth, they will be led to destruction. To "fade away" here is not so much separation from life as separation from the worldly wealth on which they depend. One can be in the prime of life and have every possession possible, and suddenly it's over in the blink of an eye. To use a parallel metaphor, life is a flickering candle that briefly brightens everything around it; then the cold winter wind comes through the open door and darkness descends. Our task is to ensure that the light of Christ continues to illumine our lives as long as possible. James calls for us to rejoice for every moment in which our short life can display Christ's light.

James has established his intended message clearly in 1:2–11. Life for every human being in this fallen world involves a series of trials or difficulties that provide obstacles to personal happiness and security. For believers, however, these trials are an opportunity to learn to rely on God more deeply and place our trust in his compassionate care. The key is to learn to endure or persevere through depending on him completely in the midst of these afflictions. The goal is to become a spiritually whole person, centered on him and at peace with the chaos around us. The rest of this first chapter elaborates on these themes and provides a transition into the rest of the letter. While James is distinctly addressing the poor in his community, all of us—rich and poor, male and female, healthy and rich, well-liked and despised—are included.

JAMES CLARIFIES THE RELATIONSHIP
BETWEEN TRIALS AND GOD (1:12–15)

In the previous ten verses (1:2–11) James introduced the key motifs of his letter—the fact of trials, the need for wisdom in overcoming them, and the basic trial behind so many of the difficulties—namely, poverty. Now in the rest of the chapter, he will expand his coverage and develop them further. He begins with trials. In 1:2–4 he showed that trials were tests of faith designed by God to teach endurance; now we will see that trials are also temptations that can seriously harm us spiritually.

The Reward for Passing the Test (1:12)

There is some question as to whether *peirasmos* in this verse means "trial," "test," as in verses 2–4, or "temptation," as in verses 13–15. If the first, it recapitulates the earlier material. If the second, it transitions into the next point. However, nearly every term in this verse goes back to the opening paragraph, so it most likely is intended to bring readers' minds back to the trials that test our faith and then to establish a contrast between the positive (testing our faith, v. 12) and negative (tempting us to disobey God, vv. 13–15). The key is how we respond to our afflictions, whether we turn to self and follow the world or turn in wisdom to follow God. The world gives fleeting pleasure that takes us down in spiritual defeat, while God gives the "perfect gift" of the new birth (1:16–18) that lifts us up to victory.

This comes to us in the form of a beatitude similar to Jesus' sayings in Matthew 5:3–12, and it speaks generally of all of us. In 1:2–4 James's emphasis was on inaugurated eschatology, the blessings that trials can introduce into our earthly lives when they lead us more directly to God. Here he emphasizes final eschatology, the heavenly reward awaiting those who overcome their earthly travails. The Greek *makarios* is found throughout the **Septuagint** (Greek Old Testament) to translate the Hebrew *'ashre* (Pss 1:1; 34:8; 40:4; Prov 8:34; Isa 56:2); both the Hebrew and Greek terms mean "fortunate, happy." But the meaning goes beyond that to embrace God's presence among his people, ensuring a divine blessing for those who rely on him. In most places, as here, I would translate, "God blesses those who ..."

Particular divine blessings here are reserved for the person
who "perseveres under trial." This verse builds on 1:2-4, which provided the command to endure, while here James looks to those who
have successfully done so. The reward belongs to them and states
that after they have "stood the test," they "will receive the crown
of life." "Test" translates the Greek *dokimos* (genuine, approved),
which is part of a primary word group used in trial passages. The
verse thus contains a double thrust, connoting both the test and
the approval that results. In 1 Peter 1:6-7 it is found twice ("proven
genuineness ... refined by fire"), referring to a divine test that is
intended to make us genuine and approved by God. Here too God
uses the trial to strengthen us spiritually and make us whole or
genuine, thereby under his approval.

This approval is especially seen in the "crown [*stephanos*] of life"
the victorious Christian is given. Most of us might think here of
the ruler's crown and picture ourselves as princes and princesses
in God's kingdom. However, this is an athletic metaphor and pictures the laurel wreath given the victorious runner in the race of
life (see 1 Cor 9:25; 1 Thess 2:19; 2 Tim 4:8; 1 Pet 5:4; Rev 2:10). The
reward is eternal life, the eternal joy earned by a life well lived.
That is the difference from athletic rewards in this life. As Paul
says in 1 Corinthians 9:25, "They do it to get a crown that will not
last, but we do it to get a crown that will last forever." I write this
as March Madness, the annual college basketball tournament, is
taking place. I think of all the Cinderella teams who have pulled
off upsets over the years, all too often lasting only a few days until
the team is defeated at the next level. In heaven it will be eternal
victory and eternal joy.

Ours is a certain reward that God has "promised to those who
love him." Certainly we don't serve God just to earn a reward for
faithful service but because we love him and it brings us real satisfaction to please him. Still, throughout the New Testament the
theme of reward is stressed. In the Sermon on the Mount, every
beatitude ends with a "for" or "because" clause spelling out the

reward for living out the ethical requirement ("Blessed are the meek, *for* they will inherit the earth," Matt 5:5). We don't live faithfully in order to get more rewards, but God wants us to know the rewards that await our service.

The Truth about Temptation (1:13–15)

As mentioned above (see comments on 1:2–4), *peirasmos* also means "temptation," and trials become temptation when we approach them in our own strength rather than relying on God. When we accept them as God-given tests and address them through prayer and trust in God, they lead to spiritual victory and divine approval. When we encounter them in our own strength and blame God for them, we fall into temptation and sin. Every trial has two possible responses, and we must make our choice. Think of a pilgrim on a quest suddenly faced with an obstacle. They can turn to God for wisdom or to self in order to get around the obstacle on their own.

A primary temptation in difficult trials is to blame God for our misfortune. So the first thing we must realize is the truth that God is not tempting us. The last line of the Lord's Prayer is best translated, "Don't let us yield to temptation" rather than "Lead us not into temptation" (Matt 6:13). God never tempts his followers. He sends trials and tests but not temptation. Rather, the trials become temptation when we fail to seek God's wisdom in handling them. In Jesus' confrontation in the wilderness (Matt 4:11), he was tested by God but tempted by Satan.

James states the reason we cannot blame God for our troubles two ways for emphasis. First, God cannot be tempted, and this genitive case (literally, "of evil") can be understood two ways: "tempted by evil" and "tempted to do evil." The thrust is probably a combination of the two. The point is that the God who cannot be tempted and who never commits evil will on the basis of his divine nature never tempt any of his people. The only connection he will ever have with evil is to condemn it and destroy it. So if we are connected at all to God, we must oppose evil and have nothing to do with it. This is stated well in 1 Corinthians 10:13: "God is faithful; he will not let you be tempted beyond what you can bear. But when you are tempted, he will also provide a way out so that you can endure it." When he sends a trial to test us, he always sends a way to endure it and the strength to rise above it.

The true source of our temptation is stated in James 1:14: "each person is tempted when they are dragged away by their own evil desire and enticed." Temptation comes from within, not from God. "Desire" refers to a self-centered longing for what we ourselves want rather than a concern for what God wants for us. John Calvin says it well: "As the inclination and excitement to sin are inward, in vain does the sinner seek an excuse from an external impulse. ... It ensnares us by its allurements, and ... it draws us away, each of which is sufficient to render us guilty."[4] In other words, we cannot blame God for our troubles; we can only blame ourselves.

"Evil" is not in the Greek but is implicit in the context. Our desires are neutral, but when they draw us away from God they become evil, and that is the connotation here. Behind James's discussion is the Jewish doctrine of the two *yetzerim*, or impulses: the tendency to do good (*yetzer hatob*) and the tendency to do evil (*yetzer hara'*). The two together constitute human nature, and in any action one or the other is dominant. There was considerable debate in Judaism about where the evil impulse originated. In the Apocalypse of Moses 19:33 it was said that Satan placed the poison of sin into the fruit of the tree in the garden of Eden, and the Jerusalem Targum on Genesis 3:6 stated it was created by Adam. Much later, according to the Talmud, it came to be believed that God created evil (b. Rabbah 27; b. Yoma 69b), and this became the majority opinion in rabbinic circles during the Middle Ages.

James next describes the process by which this takes place in our lives. We fall into temptation when we are "dragged away by

---

4. John Calvin, *Commentaries on the Catholic Epistles* (Grand Rapids: Eerdmans, 1948 [orig. 1551]), 289.

[our] own evil desire and enticed." These are hunting and fishing metaphors, depicting the bait that lures the fish and the hook or net that drags it away to destruction. In fishing the bait is an external force, but the destructive power of sin is internal; we destroy ourselves when we yield to an enticement that is actually produced by our own pleasure-seeking proclivities. Both the enticement and the surrender to it stem from the self.

The process continues in verse 15. After we are caught in the nets of deception by our own desire for pleasure, temptation leads to sin and then to total destruction. Now James turns to birth metaphors to describe it: "after desire has conceived, it gives birth to sin; and sin, when it is full-grown, gives birth to death." The cycle of life provides a perfect picture of what happens, moving from conception to birth and then to adulthood when the cycle repeats itself with parenthood. The seed of sin is planted, and self-centered desire (*epithymia*) causes it to conceive. It then bears a child, sin, which then grows to adulthood and is nourished by self. Sin, full-grown, then bears its own child, death.

The imagery here stems from the theme in Wisdom literature of the seductress who leads God's people into spiritual adultery; see particularly the immoral woman of Proverbs 5–9, whose mouth seems sweet as honey (Prov 5:3) but is filled with deadly poison (5:4–5). The only solution is to turn to wisdom, which provides God's understanding and brings victory (Prov 5:1; 7:4; 8:1, 11, 12; 9:1–6, 10–12). One must choose the path of life and refuse to follow the path of death. Revelation 17 builds on this idea, speaking of the "great prostitute" who seduces the nations and leads them into the wrath of God. Romans 5:12 is another famous verse on the effects of sin: with sin, death entered the world and came to every person.

Death is embryonic in each temptation. When we yield to temptation, it conceives and gives birth to sin, and death then takes over. Desire here is depicted as nourishing and guiding the growth to adulthood. It is a force that first gives birth to sin and then enables it to grow to adulthood. The person, born in sin, continues to feed on self-centered desires until they are full-grown. The cycle is complete when full-blown sin produces its own child, death. James pictures this in its starkest form, and at first glance it seems inevitable. Yet it is clear the inevitability comes only when one is on the wrong path. Temptation does not have to lead to sin; when tempted we can turn to God and his wisdom, thereby attaining victory.

GOD WANTS TO GIVE PERFECT GIFTS (1:16–18)

After tracing the human side of the sin cycle, James now turns to the divine side, God's desire to give only "good and perfect" gifts to his people. He never tempts (1:13) and always does only what is best for his saints. Verse 16 acts as a transition verse, common in New Testament exhortation (1 Cor 6:9, 15:33; Gal 6:7; 1 John 1:8). This warning against self-deception is what is called a present-tense prohibition and should be translated, "Do not at any time be misled." Some in this Jewish-Christian community were being deceived by their terrible struggle with poverty and persecution into thinking that God was not truly a good God and was being overly harsh with them. James obviously wants to clear up this misconception.

He calls his readers "my dear brothers and sisters" (*adelphoi mou agapētoi*), wanting them to know his depth of loving concern for them and the fact that they are all members of God's family. The stress is on God's active involvement in our lives and the necessity of our response to that. We must at all times be aware both of God's presence and of the temptations trying to lead us away from him. The great danger is that we inadvertently take the wrong path and wander (mislead ourselves[5]) away from God, thus leaving ourselves open to temptation and sin.

---

5. This middle force is better than passive ("be misled") because the temptation in 1:13–15 stems from within rather than from outside forces like Satan.

The actual truth is stated clearly in verse 17. "From above," that is, from God in heaven, come only good things. "Every good and perfect gift" is actually "all good giving [giving in general] and every [individual] perfect gift,"[6] meaning every single thing God gives is good and perfect for us. In times of trial, we have a choice to make. If we turn to self, we begin the terribly destructive cycle of sin and death. If we turn to God, we are choosing his providential care and will discover the truth that "*in all things* God works for the good of those who love him" (Rom 8:28).

In this process he gives only "good and perfect" gifts, demonstrated especially in Luke 11:13, where he gives the greatest gift of all, the Holy Spirit, "to those who ask him." This builds on the idea of James 1:4—the "good and perfect" gift, which includes the trial of our faith, makes us "perfect and whole" (NIV: "mature and complete"). It is often thought that James is particularly thinking of the gift of divine wisdom (1:5), but trials are gifts in themselves, and I believe James is thinking broadly here. So both the process (trials as God's good gift) and the product (spiritual wholeness) are perfect for us. This does not mean they are always pleasant, happy experiences. All too often they are accompanied by pain and hardship (see Heb 12:11), but they are always best for us and perfect in the sense that they result in spiritual maturity.

The source of all this is the One "from above"; the Greek *anōthen*, used here, also appears in John 3:3, where it describes the new birth. Every good thing we have in life is actually not earthly but heavenly in origin, "coming down" to us like the new Jerusalem in Revelation 21:2 (also Gal 4:26). The source is further identified here as "the Father of the heavenly lights," a description found only here in Scripture and uniting two Jewish ideas—God as the Lord of creation (Job 38:2–7) and as Father of the universe,

---

6. There is also a poetic air in the rhythm of the Greek, which may mean this was a creedal saying in the early church.

whose sovereign power is seen in the fact that he "made the great lights" of the heavens (Ps 136:7).

This Lord of creation "does not change like shifting shadows." More literally, this could be translated "with whom there is no variation or shadow of turning" (NKJV). It draws a contrast between the constantly shifting lights of the night sky and the immutable God. There are two ways of understanding the imagery. James could be saying that God renders the astral forces (the stars as demonic powers) powerless and by doing so liberates people to find the strength to handle their trials; or this could mean more simply that God is sovereign over his created universe and controls the movement of the stars. The latter is more likely in this context. The point is that God does not change (Ps 102:27; Mal 3:6), that he can be counted on to be in charge of his world. His perfect gifts for us are always best for us, and we can rely on him.

Finally, James points to the greatest of gifts along with the Spirit, the gift of new birth (Jas 1:18). This immutable God "chose to give us birth through the word of truth." As we seek his divine wisdom, he gives to us even more—his word of unchanging truth. There is some difference of understanding regarding the birth imagery here. Some see it as a reference to God's creating humankind in the first place; others, to his gift of eternal life, his redemptive work in providing spiritual rebirth. The first option would best fit a Jewish document, but since this is a Christian work, the spiritual rebirth option is a better fit.

The term for "chose" (boulētheis) does not refer to divine election but means that God decided to exercise his will and gave us freely his eternal truth so that we could experience birth to eternal life. He created a new community, a messianic people as an outlet for his love. Yet we chose to rebel and exercise our freedom through Adam to sin against God (Rom 5:12). The metanarrative of Scripture then tells how God lovingly brought us back to him by sacrificing his Son on the cross so we could experience forgiveness of sin and new life. When we come to faith in Christ, that is the new birth described here, the greatest gift we will ever know.

The means by which we receive this is "the word of truth," a descriptive genitive (= "his true word") for the gospel message (2 Cor 6:7; Eph 1:13; 2 Tim 2:15), which confronts sinners with God's salvation and brings them to new life in Christ. God spoke, and the first creation took place (Gen 1:3, 6, 9, 14, 20, 24). Now he has spoken again, and the new creation has come into being.

The result of this new birth is that we become "a kind of first-fruits of all he created." This idea of the new birth as firstfruits continues the creation motif found elsewhere in this section, speaking of the gleanings of the harvest that were seen as a harbinger or promise of fruitfulness yet to come. It was used in the sacrificial system (Exod 23:16; Lev 23:10–11; Deut 14:23), of Christ's resurrection as guaranteeing ours (1 Cor 15:20, 23), and of the first converts in a region (Rom 16:5; 1 Cor 16:15). Here it looks at Christ followers as the new creation of God and an early promise of converts yet to come. As God's harvest, we become a special part of his new creation. So we are all firstfruits, meant to be a harbinger of God's salvific blessing, consecrated, holy, and special in his sight.

———

The first issue James addresses in his letter is trials of faith (vv. 2–4), which are defined as tests from God purposed to bring his people to maturity. James begins with a seemingly ridiculous command to "consider it pure joy" as we pass through difficult times, but the key is to look at it from God's perspective rather than ours. When we realize the true significance of a trial, as in the testing of God's Son in the wilderness in Matthew 4, we can rejoice because God's presence in our lives is more real than ever. As with God's leaders throughout Scripture, trials may produce spiritual growth.

What we need to teach us perseverance and help us grow is wisdom (vv. 5–8). When we lack it (which is most of the time), we must go to God, for he is the only true source of wisdom. Yet when we do so, we must remember that he is always there for us, always responsive to our prayers, and always doing what is best for us. No problem can arise that he cannot turn around for our good (Rom 8:28). He will enable us to turn our trials into benefits in the long run. Yet when we pray, we dare not "doubt," meaning to be divided between trusting God and living for the world. We might call those who do this "spiritual surfers," for they follow every wave of life up and down. They are totally unstable as they flit between God and the world. They want God to do very little, for they are too busy living for their pleasures. So God lets them live the way they want and does not involve himself in their lives. No wonder it all descends into chaos and misery for them. But they have brought it on themselves.

Then James applies it all to the issue of rich and poor in the world and in the kingdom of God (vv. 9–11). Poverty is certainly one of the most prevalent trials, with the high numbers of poor in this world and the social stratification that governs nearly everything. The point here is that the marginalized status of the poor should disappear in the church. The rich ought to rejoice in the fact that God is taking their earthly status and lowering it in his community, and that both God and the wealthy themselves are elevating the place of poor Christians among God's people, as indeed will be the case in eternity. The place of the poor among God's people should be immensely higher than in the world, and they should be the focus of attention instead of being the forgotten people. The rich glory in the fact that they can work to alleviate the afflictions and raise the poor to a position equal to them in church and kingdom. Then the rich can join God in that equalizing force in this sinful world.

James continues with a promise (v. 12), saying that those who stand the test will receive at the final judgment the "crown of life" as an eternal reward for their faithfulness. The process of temptation (vv. 13–15) contrasts the victory of endurance. God is not to blame, for he never tempts us; only self and Satan tempt us. James uses birth imagery for sin and temptation, picturing the trial as the seed that is nourished by self, grows up, and produces its child, sin, which itself matures and bears its own child, death. It is clear that we have only ourselves to blame for our spiritual failures.

In contradistinction to self, which turns trials into temptation and leads us into sin and then to death, stands the "good and perfect gift" from God (vv. 16–18). This includes both the trials themselves as well as their result: spiritual growth and victory. God, when he sends trials, does so because they are the very gift we need.

The implications are enormous. When we face difficulties, we must make certain we respond not from our own strength but turn to God and embrace his gift of the test that will prove perfect for us as we learn to rely on him. The wondrous thing is that we are dealing with the unchangeable God who made the heavens, and so it is the God of creation who stoops down to lift us up in the midst of our hardships.

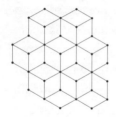

HEARING AND DOING THE WORD
(1:19–27)

The first eighteen verses introduced the major themes of this letter, and now 1:19–2:26 is an immensely practical section that defines the true meaning of wisdom: it is not just a matter of thinking the right thoughts or speaking the right words but involves doing the right things. James opens by expanding on the "word of truth" (v. 18), saying that we have not truly listened to it until we have acted on what we have heard (1:19–27). Later, he will use three temptations as examples: improper speech (1:19–27), discrimination against the poor (2:1–13), and faith without works (2:14–26).

Wisdom is a dynamic process, a life-oriented mindset as the believer lives out God's demands through daily deeds. It is not just our thought life or what we claim is true but how we act out these thoughts and claims in our practical life. This section is a serious warning against a half-hearted Christianity that listens to divine truths and appears interested but is unwilling to act on them. As 1:27 makes clear, "pure and faultless" Christianity is intensely practical and proves itself by demonstrating our internal understanding through external obedience.

This opening section (vv. 19–27) establishes the basic message: it is not enough to hear God's truths; until we have "put them into practice," we have not truly listened (Matt 7:24). A proper response will always involve the type of obedient lifestyle that proves we were truly listening. It is one thing to *talk* a good game, quite a different thing actually to *play* a good game. God demands the latter.

JAMES GIVES THREE ETHICAL COMMANDS (1:19)

James begins with three characteristics of what we may call "people of the word," those who truly center their lives on God's principles for a proper walk with Christ. This provides not just the thesis of this section but another major emphasis of the book as a whole. It introduces everything that follows. The Greek *iste*[1] could be a statement ("This you know," NASB) referring to catechetical material they had previously been taught, or an imperative ("know this," most other translations). This latter option better fits the exhortation style of this section, referring to essential information they must heed. Thus the NIV "take note of this" fits very well.

Life's difficulties will always provoke response, but we must be extremely careful to make it the proper response as defined in the three commands of verse 19. These stem from wisdom proverbs regarding anger and the misuse of the tongue, seen in ancient Jewish writings like Sirach 5:11 ("Be quick to listen and deliberate in giving an answer"; see also 6:33–35) or Pirqe Avot 5:12 ("There are four temperaments among students: Quick to understand and quick to forget ... slow to understand and slow to forget"). The command to pay close attention is similar to Jesus' "Whoever has ears, let them hear" (Matt 11:15; 13:9, 43; also Rev 2:7, 11, 17, 29; 3:6, 13, 22; 13:9). They must carefully heed the injunctions that follow.

The three admonitions develop a wordplay on "quick-slow," connoting a constant readiness and openness to listen carefully before speaking, first to God and then to those around you. This is the heart of ministry, a love for others and a compassionate presence that tells others you are there for them and care deeply, that they can bare their souls and be both accepted and aided in their

---

1. A few more recent manuscripts have *hōste*, "therefore" (K P Ψ Byz), but this is later and unlikely.

needs. Listening is an act of love that is desperately needed today. "Quick to listen" is a very Jewish idea, including not only listening but also its result, acting on what is heard. When we listen to God, we will be constantly ready to heed God's commands; when we listen to others, we will be ready to help.

In contrast, our quickness to listen must involve being "slow to speak," meaning a hesitation to speak out until we are certain we have heard all God (or the other person) is saying. This exhortation anticipates chapter 3, on the problem of the tongue. Proverbs 29:20 says, "Do you see someone who speaks in haste? There is more hope for a fool than for them." Proverbs 10:19 adds, "Too much talk leads to sin. Be sensible and keep your mouth shut" (NLT; see also Prov 11:12–13; 13:3; 17:28; 18:21; 21:23). Most of us do exactly the opposite—shoot off our mouths before we understand and get it all wrong. In ministry we should never preach until we have studied the biblical text thoroughly, and in relationships we must understand a person thoroughly before giving our opinion.

The third is equally critical. James states that our speech must proceed from careful listening, not from unreasoned, quick, and angry outbursts, which lead to hurt feelings and destroyed relationships. Uncontrolled anger leads to uncontrolled speech, and the type of deep-seated rage described here tends to destroy relationships. We see this in marriage, in parent-child interaction, and in friend-to-friend relationships. To be "slow to wrath" means that we carefully check our frustrations at the door. Of course, there is such a thing as indignation, righteous anger, but that is the subject of Ephesians 4:26 rather than of James here. The quick temper is very dangerous in every relationship.

This is one of the most needed sermon series in every church. The problem is that pastors have as much trouble with this as anyone else. We are seeing an epidemic of rage in our society, not just in school shootings and serial murders but in everyday interactions as well. There is a desperate need to deal with anger at every level of church and society. Disagreement and divisiveness have split churches in every age, and we must learn to share our frustrations and help each other to handle the hurts and wrongs we go through virtually every day. This type of anger is always the by-product of a self-centered life; we must learn from God to live for others more than for ourselves.

HUMAN ANGER IS INCOMPATIBLE WITH GOD'S RIGHTEOUSNESS (1:20–21)

James develops these three injunctions in reverse order and begins with "slow to become angry." We must eschew giving way to our baser reactions because "human anger does not produce the righteousness that God desires." This is not the Pauline sense of forensic righteousness (Rom 3:21–26, being declared right with God) but the Old Testament, Jewish sense of ethical righteousness, the righteous deeds he demands of us.

One could possibly translate, "Human anger does not produce justice," and some have seen this as a response to the later Zealot movement of the 60s that led to the Jewish revolt. However, the context makes this difficult, for that was a later movement, and there is little indication of that emphasis in James. The better parallels are found in 3:9–10 (cursing others) and 5:9 (grumbling against others).

The emphasis is on the contrast between "the wrath of man [*andros*]" and "the righteousness of God"—that is, human anger and divine righteousness. The two cannot coexist, and if God is present human selfishness and rage must give way. "Of God" is what we call a general genitive, combining the descriptive (divine righteousness), the subjective (God acting in righteousness), and the objective (God receiving our righteous deeds). We must live out his righteousness and return to him all that he has done for us. So there is no room for quick-tempered responses in the Christian life.

The answer moves from the negative to the positive sides of the Christian response (1:21). Negatively, we must "get rid of all moral

filth and the evil that is so prevalent."² This is a common ethical
maxim seen also in Colossians 3:18 and Ephesians 4:22, picturing
the act of throwing away dirty clothes or clearing away sin like
overgrown weeds. "Filth" here does not depict dirty clothes that
can be washed but clothes so filthy they can only be thrown away.
So these are not simply sins to be endured and gradually cleaned
but are so morally evil that they have to be immediately discarded.
James is thinking of anger, injustice, and the sins of the tongue,
those things he has been talking about above, possibly especially a
malicious desire to hurt others. This filth contains an "abundance
of evil [NIV: 'evil that is so prevalent']" and cannot be tolerated.
We can have nothing to do with such sins.

The positive side is to "humbly accept the word planted in you,
which can save you." Humility probably modifies both halves of
the verse and describes that we both cast off sin and receive the
word in complete reliance on God. We cannot overcome the evil
controlling our lives in our own strength. James now uses an agricultural metaphor to tell us that when we rely on the Lord, we have
not only a new source of strength but also a new source of truth
to guide us. God has "planted" his word in us, and as we turn to
him, this implanted seed takes root and begins to bear fruit and
becomes a harvest of life in us, another of the perfect gifts from
God (1:17). This reminds me of Mark 4:1-20, the parable of the soils/
sower, which asks the question of us, what kind of soil are you?

James is telling us to open ourselves to the internal spiritual
power of the Word in us, listen carefully to its truths, come to
understand their meaning and message, and live out their principles in our daily life. This is another of those wonderful passages
on the value of deep Bible study. This is the reason in fact that I

---

2. Scholars are divided as to whether this verse concludes 19-20 and the sins
described there or introduces 22-27 and thus places the emphasis on "the
word." It is a transition verse, but I believe it is more closely connected to
19-20 and so place it there.

am writing this commentary series, to make it possible to do this type of Bible study on any book of the New Testament. We are to enter our study with a humble prayer that God change our lives accordingly and teach us ever-new truths to guide us.

The reason for turning to God's implanted word is that it "can save you." This is not just regeneration, for we are dealing here with the Christian life as a whole. Salvation does not just connote the new birth but is a covering term for the new life in Christ. "Can save" is actually two verbs, *dynamenon sōsai*, "able to save" or "has the power to save." Throughout our earthly lives as Christians, we are in process of experiencing the power of God's salvation as it bears a harvest of spiritual fruit in our lives. The Greek also has "save your souls" (*tas psychas hymōn*), which does not mean your soul separate from your body but your whole "self," everything you are as a person. The NIV's brief "can save you" is adequate for this interpretation. This passage points to present salvation but also to the believer's ultimate deliverance from sin and death at Christ's glorious return, also emphasized often (1:12; 2:12–13; 3:1; 4:12; 5:5, 7, 15).

BE DOERS OF THE WORD (1:22–25)

Now James develops further the first command of verse 19: "quick to listen." The command to be doers of the word also tells what it means to "accept the word planted in you" in verse 21. We have not "accepted" it merely when we listen to it. We must obey it and act out its mandates day by day. There is an ABA pattern here, with the two admonitions on practicing the word (1:22, 25) framing the illustration of the mirror (1:23–24). To open our ears to ascertain the meaning of a passage is insufficient. The true purpose of Bible study is for the whole person (the "souls" in 1:21) to be changed in every area of our lives.

This begins with a present-tense imperative stressing ongoing action: continue to be doers of the word. Some think we should retain the thrust of *ginesthe*, thus emphasizing the process of "becoming doers," but its normal thrust is synonymous with *einai*, "be doers," and that is likely. The reading of Torah was central in synagogues, with five readers on feast days, six on the Day of Atonement, and seven on Sabbaths. James's point is that God intended people to go out and practice the message of the texts that were read. This highlights the sad state of Scripture reading in our day. Many churches have no Scripture reading at all, and I have even heard some leaders say that the reason is that reading the Bible in church is boring. In many others the sermon is nothing but a pep talk devoid of much biblical content whatsoever. Both of these are abominations to God! The truth is that many of the New Testament books were designed to be read in church (see Col 4:16; 1 Tim 4:13; Rev 1:3), and it was just as precious to the early church as it was to synagogue services.

The NIV captures the doers/hearers emphasis well: "Do not merely listen to the word, and so deceive yourselves. Do what it says." There are many scriptural examples of this thrust. After Moses read the regulations of Torah in Exodus 24:3, the people responded, "Everything the LORD has said we will do." This was a frequent warning (Deut 28:58; 29:29; Josh 1:8), and in the famous meditation on God's word in Psalm 119, the poet promises often to "obey" (Ps 119:1, 59, 67, 173). Jesus said that anyone who listened without obeying is a fool (Matt 7:26), and in the Great Commission Jesus stressed teaching the nations "to obey everything I have commanded you" (Matt 28:20). In John 14:15-24 loving Jesus must always result in doing what he says, and this continues in Paul as well, as in Romans 2:13 ("those who obey … will be declared righteous"), 2 Corinthians 10:5 ("we take captive every thought to make it obedient to Christ"), and 2 Timothy 3:15-16 ("All Scripture … is useful for teaching, rebuking, correcting and training in righteousness").

Those who fail to live out the word deceive themselves because they think their own guesswork is sufficient to please God. In Colossians 2:4, this verb describes false teachers who use "fine-sounding arguments" to lead people astray. This is the height of foolishness, for sinful humankind can never understand God. God has revealed himself to us in his word, and only there do we have reliable data for pleasing God. Rationalization and self-deception are virtually part of the DNA of sin, and people left to their own devices will always get it wrong. To talk the talk without walking the walk is to be in serious danger.

There are three necessary steps, and each one must lead into the next: we must listen to and study the word, we must come to understand it in terms of its God-inspired meaning, and we must practice it in our lives. From reading to understanding to doing, we will be illuminated by the Holy Spirit if we sincerely seek God in his word.

In verses 23–24 James illustrates this with a short parable describing the kind of person who "looks intently into" the word without doing anything about it. He begins with a condition of fact that assumes the reality of the statement: "If [as is the case] someone is a hearer of the word and not a doer," or as in the NIV, "Anyone who listens to the word but does not do what it says." To James this describes all too many of those he is addressing, listening without heeding. He compares such people with an absurd person who looks at herself in a mirror, sees a mess that desperately needs to be fixed, but then just shrugs her shoulders, walks away, and immediately forgets what she had looked like.

Mirrors in the first century were made of silver for the wealthy and polished copper or bronze for regular people. They were fairly common in the first century but yielded blurry images, so one would need to "look intently" at what they saw (katanoeō = "look carefully, contemplate"). Let's modernize the picture. You get up in the morning, stumble into the bathroom, see yourself in the mirror over the sink, notice your messy hair and blotchy face, and then walk away and go to work without doing a thing and just forget what you looked like. Who in their right mind would do such a thing—go to the trouble of inspecting themselves carefully in a mirror when they don't care what they look like? That's a ridiculous scenario, even more so in our day, when there is a huge industry just for hiding every blemish on our face. How we look has become a virtually "religious" obsession in our society, so this is an even more apt illustration for us.

Now in verse 25 James applies the parable to us spiritually. God's word is the mirror of the soul and was revealed to us by God so we could see who we really are in comparison to God's picture of what we should look like. The more we look "intently" into its revealed truths, the more we see ourselves as we really are and are told how to fashion ourselves in his revealed image, the "image of God." The verb for the intense looking (*parakyptō*) refers to careful study and meditation on the meaning of the text.

He describes this spiritual mirror as "the perfect law that gives freedom." The solution to spiritual self-deception and failure is found in the very title. This law of God, the Torah of the Messiah revealed in the new covenant, does two things for us—it perfects us or brings us to maturity (see 1:4, 17), and it liberates us from the power of sin and self. James is obviously not thinking of the New Testament. His is probably the first book to have been written, and it is very doubtful that he ever saw his letter as the beginning of a new canon. That understanding was late in developing, probably beginning with the recognition of the inspired status of the Gospels and then including Paul, perhaps starting in the latter part of the first century. Still, it would have applied to the later recognition of the New Testament works.

It is difficult to ascertain the referent to the "law" here. It could be the Mosaic law, the Torah, as James was a strictly observant Jewish Christian who still observed the law. But that does not fit the larger context well, as the focus has been on God's "word" in a broader sense. At the other extreme, he might be referring to the Christian proclamation of the gospel, with "law" purely symbolic here. But the Jewish overtones of the book make that unlikely. It is best taken as a combination of the two, with the Christian gospel fulfilling the Torah message of salvation or deliverance from sin.

So the "perfect law that gives freedom" is equivalent to the "word" of 1:18, 21–23, referring to the gospel truths as the new law or covenant provided by Christ and the heart of gospel proclamation. The new covenant "Torah of the Messiah" also includes the fulfillment of the Old Testament truths in Christ and the church. This implanted word of God is "perfect" in that it performs a "perfect" or "complete" work in the believers, making them "complete" (1:4). It is also perfect because it "gives freedom" (repeated in 2:12) from the power of sin and gives them God's new salvation.

There are two actions on our part. First, we "continue" or "remain" in it,[3] meaning we continually obey the word and allow it to direct our actions. It is clear that anyone who ignores the centrality of the word in their lives and in their church is in great danger, for they have lost their spiritual GPS indicator that tells them where they are in their pilgrimage through life. We will see this danger in 5:19: "wandering from the truth."

Second, we must make certain we are "not forgetting what they have heard, but doing it" or practicing it. This describes what the life of a faithful believer who remains in Christ looks like. Such people are not "forgetful hearers" but "active doers." This obviously builds on the mirror analogy in verses 23–24, depicting such as carefully investigating themselves in the mirror of the word and, refusing to forget what it reveals, eager to act on it and change their lives accordingly. The Greek describes "a doer of work" (*poiētēs ergou*), meaning they continually "work" at the Christian walk and at applying what they are told from God's word in doing so.

The result is that such Christ followers who actively live according to God's dictates "will be blessed in what they do." Many see

---

3. Interestingly, the participle *parameinas* is aorist rather than present tense, emphasizing remaining as a characteristic of the Christian life viewed as a whole. In other words, continuing to live out the gospel truths becomes a basic part of our whole life.

this as the future or final blessing in eternity (seen in the future "will be"), but I don't think we should ignore the fact that the blessing does not come *after* they react this way but occurs *in* (*en*) the very act of doing it. Spiritual growth is its own reward. In other words, there is an inaugurated sense in what is promised here. The emphasis is on the current reward of a life well lived in the here and now, and this present blessing will end with the eternal rewards that are ours when we get to heaven. Moreover, the blessing is both inward, a personal joy and satisfaction in doing what God wants, and upward, a blessing from God expressing his pleasure in us.

JAMES CALLS THE CHURCH TO TRUE RELIGION (1:26-27)

WHAT IT IS NOT (1:26)

These verses develop the final of the commands in verse 19, "slow to speak," depicting the kind of people who "consider themselves religious" but prove themselves irreligious as a result of their big mouths. They "seem" (*dokei*; NIV: "consider") or have the outward appearance of people who worship God and follow him. They are characterized by head religion rather than heart religion and would be called "hypocrites." The term for "religious/religion" (*thrēskos/thrēskeia*) centers on the external aspect of ritual religion, the way people perceive others based on observing the outward forms, the religious acts they perform.

In particular, one can tell that their claims are a sham because they don't "bridle" or "keep a tight rein on their tongues." The analogy of a horse's bridle is quite apt, as it describes the bit placed in the horse's mouth to control where you want it to go. Controlling one's speech was always a key for a wise person in the ancient world. The "tongue" of a foolish person would be like an untamed horse racing pell-mell through the fields and in danger of running over anyone who got in its way. As such, this points forward to James 3, on the danger of the tongue. The emphasis is general here. Specific kinds of evil speech will be presented later—angry speech, slander, careless or flippant speech.

People who give in to such temptation "deceive themselves, and their religion is worthless." What emerges from the mouth is a clear sign of what truly fills the heart. These people often sincerely believe they are right with God and are headed for eternal reward. They are lying to themselves, for what they say reveals who they really are. As in Matthew 7:21–23, they may claim to have prophesied and cast out demons in Jesus' name, but their "fruit" has revealed the truth, and Jesus will say to them, "I never knew you. Away from me, you evildoers!"

Their religion has been shown to be "worthless" (*mataias*), "empty, fruitless, devoid of meaning, in vain." There is no substance to such a claim, for God and worship are far from those hypocrites' minds. In a very real sense, there is no "religion" at all, just pretense. Let me use an example—television preachers. There are many good ones, and it actually seems fairly easy to spot the fakes (their lavish lifestyles alone will prove that), but thousands of people are fooled by them. We all need to be more discerning and allow the Spirit to guide us carefully in whom we follow. All too much of God's resources are being given over to those who are living for themselves rather than the Lord. James is calling for vigilance and discernment to guide the church.

What It Is (1:27)

In place of this false, empty religion, James urges his readers to develop a walk with God that he deems as "pure and faultless." There is an interesting mixture of imagery here. As in the "religion" of verse 26, the two adjectives stem from Old Testament ritual: "pure" points to the purity laws, and "faultless," to those who are ritually clean and fit to approach God in worship. Yet at the same time this introduces the realm of ethical conduct, which will come to the fore in chapter 2. The ritual or cultic side of the

Christian life cannot be separated from the ethical or moral aspect. The two must cohere. True worship demands practical behavior (2 Tim 2:22; Heb 7:26; 1 Pet 1:4, 22). Moreover, this conduct will be done "in the sight of God the Father" (NIV: "that God our Father accepts"), who judges without partiality (1 Pet 1:17). It is God, not us, who determines what behavior is acceptable.

Religious expression that is nothing but ritual is nothing, period. As James has said repeatedly, hearing and so-called worshipping without doing—that is, living out the worship in actual service to others—is empty and meaningless. When we serve others, we are also serving God (the Greek term *latreia* means "service" that is "worship"; see Rom 12:1), and that is a necessary form of true worship (as here).

James uses two illustrations: both needs in his own community, and both strongly emphasized in the Old Testament. The first is "to look after orphans and widows in their distress." The Greek commands us to "visit" them (*episkeptesthai*), not only to take care of them but also to go to them and spend time with them. It was often used of God's "visiting" his people to deliver them from oppression (Gen 50:24; Exod 3:16; Ruth 1:6).

These were the two social categories most bereft of life's necessities. Widows were vulnerable in ancient society because they had no male protector, and the inheritance went to the sons rather than the mother in order to continue the family dynasty. The widow was left only with her dowry and her parental family, who often ignored her needs. Orphans were destitute because they had no family and often no one who cared. So these were the two most impoverished groups in ancient society (see 1 Kgs 17:8–24; 2 Kgs 4:1–7), and God commanded special attention be given them (Exod 22:22; Deut 27:19; Isa 1:17, 23; Jer 7:6; Ezek 22:7; Zech 7:10).

Their "distress" depicts the suffering and affliction they experience day by day. Social justice is a necessary, not peripheral, aspect of serving God. The saddest aspect of the modern church is the fact that all too often the examples of injustice that appear in news reports stem from churches and religious groups. We should be the solution, but all too frequently we are the problem. In many ways, a successful church is not judged by its size but by its color. A lily-white church in a region of mixed races is in a very real sense a failure in God's eyes. All too often it exists in a community deeply prejudiced against people of color!

At the same time, the external social concern must be paralleled by an internal spiritual concern. Many churches are the opposite of those described in the preceding paragraph. They have so emphasized the social side that the gospel is virtually missing from their church and denomination. So it is also necessary "to keep oneself from being polluted by the world." The adjective itself means "unspotted, unstained, without fault" and is synonymous with "pure" above. External actions must exist alongside an internal character that pleases God. The "world" (also in 2:5; 3:6; 4:4) refers to the sinful realm that surrounds us and keeps us from God. This is the definition of holiness, to be *a part of* the world and yet live a life that is *apart from* the world.

These two sides of a proper Christian lifestyle must coexist and supplement each other. Internal purity is balanced by external good deeds. We live out our dedication to the Lord by helping others, and God's love and concern for the needy is reflected in the way we conduct ourselves in the world.

———

The one thing that all human beings, whatever their social status, have in common is the ups and downs of life. Every human being lives an uncertain life, filled with trials and temptations, and even billionaires must depend on God in the day-to-day situations that test us to the utmost.

The rest of this chapter (vv. 19–27) tells us how we go about finding this victory over self and temptation—namely, by hearing and doing what God tells us. The three questions of verse 19 provide the foundation for the rest of the letter, commanding us to listen carefully before we speak and to refuse to allow anger to rule us. He develops them in reverse order, beginning with the third, slow to anger (vv. 20-21). Here we should seek God's righteousness and listen to his word rather than allow our emotions to take over as we relate to those around us.

Then he develops the first injunction, "quick to listen" (vv. 22-25), emphasizing that true listening always involves putting what we hear into practice in our lives. Hearing without doing is completely opposed throughout Scripture, and James compares it to studying your face in a mirror and then doing nothing about what you see. Such is impractical and foolish. The word of God is the mirror of the soul, and we study it to see what we need to change in our lives. The truth is that only the word of God is "perfect" for us, leading us to spiritual maturity and liberating us from sin and self via the new birth and the new life in him.

Finally, James develops the second mandate of verse 19, "slow to speak," in verses 26-27, when he challenges us to "keep a tight rein on our tongues" and develop a pure religion in our lives. We need to control what we say and make sure our lives are guided by a practical, "pure religion" that cares for the disadvantaged like orphans and widows. We should not talk a good walk until we have lived a good walk, proved by the way we care for those who have little in life. To live a life "unstained by the world," we must give of ourselves for the needy in our world.

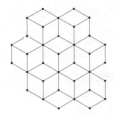

THE SIN OF FAVORITISM
IN THE ASSEMBLY
(2:1–13)

I n 1:2–11 the three basic themes of the book were presented—trials and tests, the need for wisdom, and the specific problem of poverty. This is followed by a practical section detailing three examples that depict how these are applied to the Christian life, first by the need to add obedience and good deeds to hearing the word (1:19–27), second in avoiding favoritism of the rich over the poor in the Christian community (2:1–13), and third in making certain that faith ensues in good works (2:14–26).

The demand to care for orphans and widows in 1:27 is the polar opposite of the sin of favoritism here in 2:1–7. God's people must elevate the poor and take care of them, so when Christians discriminate against the poor in their communities, it is particularly heinous. To favor the rich and look down on the poor, they are acting against the "perfect law" that is intended to liberate rather than humiliate the needy (1:25, see also Rom 2:11; Eph 6:9; Col 3:25).

JAMES PROHIBITS PREJUDICE (2:1–7)

Thesis: The Sin of Discrimination (2:1)

Once more (see 1:2, 16, 19) James addresses his readers as "my brothers and sisters" so they will know that his admonition is an expression of love for members of his Christian family. He does not want to see them indicted by his and their heavenly Father. This is especially appropriate since he is pleading for them to show brotherly love to the poor in their congregations and communities. They must realize that faith and favoritism cannot cohere.

There are three ways to translate this—as an interrogative expecting the answer "no" ("You aren't showing favoritism, are you?"), as a prohibition (NET: "do not show prejudice if you have faith"), or as a statement (NIV: "how can you claim to have faith … if you favor some people"). Grammatically, the second is the best option (as seen in the Greek *mē echete*), but the third still captures the meaning well. As a present-tense imperative the emphasis is, "Do not at any time show prejudice." The meaning of *prosōpolēmpsia* is "receiving someone according to their face" or external looks, but it applies to every type of favoritism—riches, power, fame, looks, and so on. "Faith" here means trust in the Lord Jesus, or the Christian faith.

This is particularly faith "in our glorious Lord Jesus Christ." "Glorious" is a genitive, literally "of glory." It has four possible meanings: a descriptive genitive (NIV: "in our glorious Lord"), a form stressing his exalted status ("in the glory of our Lord"), as a title ("our Lord Jesus Christ, the Glory"), or stressing his **Shekinah** presence ("faith in our Lord of glory, Jesus Christ"). Since "of glory" is last for emphasis, the fourth option here is probably best.[1] There is definitely a sense that Jesus is being portrayed as the exalted Shekinah presence of God in the community (see also Matt 9:7; Rom 9:4; 1 Cor 2:8; Heb 1:3; 2 Pet 1:17).

James is saying that you cannot claim to have faith in the exalted Jesus and be a member of his messianic community when

---

1. It is sometimes argued that this high and titular sense of "glory" was not used this early in the life of the early church, but I do not see this as true. Once it was recognized that Jesus was Yahweh, the attributes of deity would quickly have been applied to him.

you are looking down on the poor and diminishing their place in the church in favor of the wealthy. The two simply cannot exist together. Favoritism of any type obviates the claim to be the church of Christ, for if we don't feel about the poor and needy as Christ did, we are hardly Christian in that critical area of our lives. This applies to all kinds of prejudice—racial, status, or simply one's gift-edness (the smart kids, the athletic kids, etc.). There is a necessary egalitarian atmosphere in Christ's communities that must reflect Christ's attitudes to the rich diversity of people in God's creation.

ILLUSTRATION: FAVORING THE RICH IN THE WORSHIP SERVICE (2:2–4)

James constructs a hypothetical situation illustrating economic prejudice in order to make his point. Nevertheless, it was a very real possibility, for while the early church contained a strong majority of poor people and slaves, there were still numerous examples of the wealthy, like Zacchaeus (Luke 19), or the two who buried Jesus, Nicodemus and Joseph of Arimathea (John 19). This likely does depict actual situations in James's churches, but he is nevertheless presenting it as hypothetical.

Scholars have posited two possible scenarios for the story. Traditionally it has been seen as a Christian worship service, with "synagogue" (NIV, NLT translate it "meeting") reflecting the Jewish-Christian background. However, a rival understanding has recently become popular, seeing this as a Jewish law court. (Synagogues had that function at the local level.) The scholars who posit this scenario argue that a worship setting would use *ekklēsia*, so this was more likely a judicial courtroom, reflecting Leviticus 19:15: "do not show partiality to the poor or favoritism to the great, but judge your neighbor fairly."[2] It is possibly also reminiscent of 1 Corinthians 6:2, where the judicial courts are urged to solve church issues.

---

2. See also Deuteronomy Rabbah 5:6; b. Shevu'ot 31a; t. Sanhedrin 6:2.

Both are viable, but the worship setting makes the best sense as the more natural reading of the language. The term "synagogue" was used by Jewish Christian house churches well into the second century. The image of seating people would fit either scenario, but the traditional understanding is slightly preferable. The believer in this case is ushering the wealthy visitor to the best seat in the assembly.

One of the visitors is quite wealthy. It could be a woman dressing this way (see 1 Tim 3:9; 1 Pet 3:3), but in that culture it would more likely have been a man. The wealth is shown by the "gold ring and fine clothes," literally "gold-ringed and with shining clothes." Garments dyed scarlet or purple were especially expensive because of the difficult process involved in making them. At the same time a poverty-stricken individual enters "in filthy old clothes." The clothes are dirty because this person is shoddy and destitute, forced to wear the same outfit every day. James at this stage is not telling us whether the two opposites are believers; that will be decided later.

The fact that the person has to be escorted to a seat shows he is not a regular but a guest. Because he has wealth and status, he is given "special attention" and "a good seat." All should be treated equally and with respect, but only the person with the fancy clothes is shown any regard. Possibly hoping for favors later, the usher, who is supposed to be "slow to speak" (1:19), speaks right up and tells him to sit in the best seat in the house.

After fawning on the rich man, he then says with complete disregard to the poor person, "You stand there," or "Sit on the floor." To be forced to stand far away from the podium is to be treated as an outsider, and the irony is that the wealthy visitor is the actual outsider and the poor person is likely the actual member of the church. Yet the distinguished one gets to sit "here" (*su kathou ōde*, "you sit here"), and the downtrodden one has to stand "there." Moreover, to sit on the floor literally "under my footstool" is to be treated as a slave sitting at the feet of the church official, like the

Messiah's enemies in Psalm 110:1 ("Make your enemies a footstool for your feet"). The favoritism could not be more obvious.

The conclusion is absolutely correct (2:4): "have you not discriminated among yourselves and become judges with evil thoughts?" They have become evil judges, while in 4:11–12 there is to be "only one Lawgiver and Judge," and in Matthew 7:1 it says, "Do not judge, or you too will be judged." The Greek "discriminate" is *diekrithēte*, used in 1:6 for those with "divided minds" between God and this world. Here too their loyalty is mixed between calling themselves Christians but acting like pagans. To be divided between rich and poor is to be divided between following God and following the world. The double-minded heart toward the Lord is caused by divisive conduct in the church. In fact, we are told that this discrimination is "among yourselves" (*en heautois*), which makes it a corporate sin of the whole church when such practices are allowed.

Moreover, they have become "judges [*kritai*] with evil thoughts [or motives]." Their whole way of thinking has become corrupted (against 1:27, "keep oneself from being polluted by the world"). The idea of their "thought life" probably combines both their inner thinking and their outward communication to others. What they think and how they speak are both affected. There are three steps— what they think affects how they speak, and that determines how they act. In this case all three are guided by the "evil" that possesses them. Favoritism of any kind—social (as here), racial, or simply on the basis of externals (looks, athletics, intellect, and so on)—is worldly and the product of sin in the world. Certainly our society has proved beyond all doubt the utter devastation caused by human prejudice.

QUESTIONING THE INCONSISTENCY (2:5–7)

The incongruity of favoring the rich over the poor in flagrant disregard of God's clear mandate to care for the unfortunate is brought out by four questions, all expecting the answer "yes." The first two center on the poor, the latter two on the rich. Calling

them "brothers and sisters" for the fifth time to stress the love that
lies behind this challenge (1:2, 16, 19; 2:1), James introduces it by
reminding them of Jesus' frequent challenge: "Whoever has ears to
hear, let them hear" (Mark 4:9, 23; Matt 11:15; 13:9, 43). Behind this
is the earlier mandate that to listen is to obey (1:19–22). It is time to
stop the sin of prejudice once for all. Alertness and spiritual vigilance in this area must lead to a changed lifestyle. James is turning from the specific situation of favoritism in the worship service
to the general "laws" governing all such types of discrimination.

His first point calls for them to acknowledge that yes, God has
indeed "chosen the poor in this world to be rich in faith." The "poor
in this world" could be possessive ("the world's poor"), sphere ("the
poor in this world"), or reference ("poor in the eyes of the world,"
NIV). This third is likely best and shows what people value in this
life and means that the poor are judged as inferior by the worldly
(including many Christians) around them. In the "carnal" opinion formed as a result of this prejudiced world system, the poor
are degraded in worth even though God has given them the privilege of heavenly riches by leading them to greater faith in him on
the basis of their circumstances. What they lose in earthly status
they more than gain in heavenly status.

The marginalized are the subjects of God's special election
(*exelexato*), meaning they have a special place in his economy
because of the "faith" they have learned from their trials, and
so he has elevated them to special status in the community as
spiritual leaders (1:9, the special "honor" reserved for the downtrodden). The question is, which is more important, the world's
resources or God's resources? The answer is certainly obvious, but
even Christians rarely (if ever) actually think or live this way. The
truth is that, as we will see, these Christians prefer the very rich
who have oppressed them and slandered the name of Jesus (2:6–7),
just because they are rich.

Paul makes the same point in 1 Corinthians 1:27–28 to the opin-
ionated and biased Corinthians that "God chose the weak things

of the world to shame the strong." Those who have nothing in this world are made the upper class of heaven in the sphere of faith. The first beatitude of Matthew 5:3 states that the "poor in spirit" have received "the kingdom of heaven." The NLT translates this, "God blesses those who are poor in spirit and realize their need for him." They have no earthly resources to counter their desperate situations and so must turn entirely to God and depend on him. As a result, they discover spiritual riches. Luke 12:21 speaks of being "rich toward God," which is vastly superior to earthly riches.

Not only are the poor rich in faith; they are also heirs of God's promises. It is the poor who will "inherit the kingdom he promised those who love him." This builds on the remnant idea, with the poor who have little of the world's goods destined to have eternal reward. The inheritance motif is a central teaching of Scripture. They don't just have a place in God's kingdom but an inheritance. The Romans were very careful about laws of inheritance. Two-thirds of the estate went to the older brother to guarantee the family dynasty continued. To God the poor who have spent their lives centering on him had an eternal future promised to them. The great reversal at the end of history would center on them.

The inheritance theme began with the promise to Abraham and the patriarchs that they would inherit the promised land (Lev 20:24; Deut 1:8) and later came to be used of the kingdom blessings given by God to his people (Ps 16:5; Dan 12:13). Jesus used it of the **eschatological** promises that his followers would inherit the earth (Matt 5:5; 25:34) and eternal life (Mark 10:17). Paul spoke often of our inheritance (Rom 8:17; Gal 5:21; Eph 1:14, 18), and it is particularly predominant in Hebrews (1:2, 4, 14; 6:12, 17; 9:15; 11:7–8; 12:17). God will make up the deprivations the poor have endured in eternity, but this is to begin with the way the church treats them. The kingdom is theirs in the here and now as well as in heaven, and they should be treated as such.

An important aspect of this passage is the idea that these things are "promised those who love him" (see also 1:12), which would include the faithful who refuse to discriminate as well as the poor themselves. The "kingdom" as God's reign has already arrived, yet it will not be finalized until the **eschaton** (end). The promises are absolutely certain, and they are to guide our lives in the present as well as our future hope. By the very fact that the poor have to depend entirely on God at all times, they have a special love relationship with him. One of the terrible things they often have to go through is being despised by their own church people, but they have the Lord, his love, and the promises to comfort them in these dark hours.

The second pair of questions is directed to the rich (2:6–7). God's people have "dishonored the poor," meaning they have sinned by insulting and shaming them. God has chosen the poor to be his special possession, but these people by favoring the wealthy have shown them little but contempt. Moreover, the very people these Christians have preferred because of their wealth have both oppressed the Christian poor and dragged them into court.

The incongruity of it all is staggering. The members of this Jerusalem house church have on the one hand brought their own fellow members to shame and then turned around and on the other hand heaped honor on their enemies. And all just because their enemies were rich and their friends were poor! The wealthy oppressing the poor is found often in Scripture (Isa 58:6; Ezek 18:12–13; Amos 4:1; Zech 7:10), so they should have recognized the temptation right off. "Oppress" is *katadynasteuousin*, a present-tense verb denoting ongoing activity. The verb can also mean to "exploit," depicting a set of situations like 5:1–6, when wealthy landowners were cheating their field hands of proper pay so they could live in luxury.

Not only do these people steal what little money these poor Christians possess; they also drag them into court, perhaps combining the physical (hauling them in chains) with the legal (bringing up of charges). This could refer to any of several possible scenarios, from collecting debts and throwing them into debtor's prison to taking their homes for nonpayment of usury rates of interest to hauling them before the tribunals in synagogues (which functioned as the local lawcourt in most towns) like Paul did in Acts 9:1-2. In fact, all three could be in James's mind. The misuse of lawcourts is often condemned by the prophets—for instance, Amos 5:7 ("turn justice into bitterness," also 5:10-12) or Isaiah 10:2 ("deprive the poor of their rights and withhold justice," also Isa 1:17; 29:21; 59:9, 11, 15).

Moreover, the second question shows that these wealthy Jews not only afflict the Christian poor; they also "slander Jesus Christ, whose noble name you bear" (2:7 NLT). The term for "slander" is *blasphēmousin*, so these prejudiced Christians are not just bad-mouthing Jesus but actually participating in blasphemy against the Godhead. It is Christ's "noble name [they] bear" that is mocked, and out of their foolishness these people slander that "noble name" of their eternal Lord and King. This could be inadvertent sin, committed just because of the favoritism they are showing, but it could also be literal, with these foolish believers joining in the mockery of Christ by maligning their poverty-stricken fellow members of the church in order to kowtow favor with these rich people.

James is reminding them that they have taken the very name of Christ (perhaps they are already embracing the name "Christian," Acts 11:26), and the fact that they bear his "noble/good" name points to ownership, that they are God's special possession (Num 6:27; 2 Chr 7:14; Isa 43:7; 63:19; Jer 14:9). Some read a baptismal context into this, when the name of Christ was invoked over the initiate, but that is speculative. The emphasis is on the fact that they belong to God and are members of his family. When they allow Christ's name to be insulted and join in insulting his followers, they are in serious trouble with God.

JAMES POINTS TO THE ROYAL LAW OF LOVE (2:8–13)

This entire section (2:1-13) centers on the issue of favoritism. The first part (vv. 1-7) deals with the "what"—that discrimination of any type breaks God's laws and endangers our faith. The next two sections (vv. 5-7, 8-11) deal with the "why"—it is contrary to God's will for the poor (v. 5); it is illogical because these wealthy are enemies of God's people (vv. 6-7); and it is against Scripture and the royal law of love (vv. 8-11). Simply put, prejudice and favoritism break God's law and are opposed to scriptural truth.

The Royal Law Stated (2:8-9)

James presents a conditional sentence to stress our responsibility: "If you really keep the royal law ... you are doing right." James calls it the "royal law" in keeping with what has been said before in 1:25-27: "the perfect law that gives freedom," and "religion that God our Father accepts as pure and faultless." God demands a faithful people who recognize truth and live it. There are two ways to take this sentence, based on whether we translate the particle *mentoi* as negative ("however," the usual thrust, as NASB, NET, REB, LEB) or positive ("yes, indeed" or "if you really," as NIV, NLT, NRSV, ESV). The former sees a contrast with the preceding description in verse 6, "you have dishonored the poor ... [but] if you really keep the royal law"). However, that is clumsy here, and the positive makes more sense, as in the NIV.

The actual contrast is seen in verses 8-9: "If you really keep the royal law ... but if you show favoritism." There are questions regarding the exact referent to the "royal law." Is it the Torah of the old covenant or the new law, the Torah of the Messiah fulfilled by Christ? If this were a Jewish document the former would be correct, but James is a Jewish Christian, so it is almost certainly the latter. A second question is whether this is specifically the love command cited from Leviticus 19:18 or is more generally the Torah as a whole combining both covenants. Most likely, "royal law" refers to all the teaching of Torah rather than one specific command, but still the love command is highlighted. Leviticus 19:18 is the apex of the ethical side of the law and sums up the issue here.

The fact that the new law is "royal" does not just mean it is supreme over all others but means it is the law of the "kingdom" and comes from the "king" over all. The laws are kingly in essence and liberating in effect (1:27). "If you really keep" is literally, "If you fulfill" (*ei teleite*), and means God's people are meant to complete his law by obeying it. When they discriminate, they are not just breaking his laws but denying their place in God's kingdom by doing so.

The Leviticus command to "love your neighbor as yourself" is actually phrased as a "Thou shalt" imperative, a divine or eternal command. In Leviticus the "neighbor" is especially fellow Israelites but also includes foreigners in the land (Lev 19:33–34). The command here is as broad as possible, including both believers and unbelievers, as in Galatians 6:10: "do good to all people, especially to those who belong to the family of believers." Moreover, you must love them "as yourself," meaning that you care as deeply for them as you do yourself. As members of God's family, we are all extensions of one another, and the love we show others must be a reflection of the love we have for ourselves.

In contrast, to show favoritism is to commit a serious sin against the Lord's will, against the poor whom we are supposed to love, and against ourselves. "Show favoritism" is *prosōpolēmpteō*, "to receive someone according to their face" (see 2:1 for the noun form), showing preference to people just because they are more wealthy, more attractive, a better athlete, and so on. Here James is thinking of Leviticus 19:15: "Do not show partiality to the poor or favoritism to the great, but judge your neighbor fairly." James tells us all such is sin, and such people are guilty of breaking the law.

The term for "sin" here is *hamartia*, stressing the moral side with imagery of an archer missing the target, failing to hit God's mark. The second half is even more specific, as those who sin by showing prejudice are "convicted by the law" of being "lawbreakers." In John 16:8 the Spirit is God's prosecuting attorney, proving to the world that it stands guilty before God. That is the case here as well, and all that remains is for God to sentence them in his *bēma* (judgment seat) lawcourt. Breaking or violating God's law is a deliberate act by those who know they are sinning. Those who show partiality to the rich stand guilty before God. They "sin with a high hand" and deserve what they will receive from God the Judge.

GUILTY OF THE WHOLE LAW (2:10-11)

The "for" (*gar*) that begins 2:10 shows that these verses provide evidence that verse 9 is correct—the prejudiced truly stand before God guilty of violating his laws. We need to remember again that James and his audience are observant Jewish Christians, so he is proving their guilt by appealing now to the complete unity of the Torah. To break one divine injunction is to be guilty of them all. They may consider prejudice just a small, unimportant sin, but it is just as serious as the Ten Commandments. The laws he cites come from the Decalogue, but that is because they form the heart and soul of the Torah as a whole, and indeed of the entire Old Testament. Those who discriminate are not partial lawbreakers but stand wholly condemned by God. So they may "keep" the rest of the law assiduously, yet they are still guilty.

Literally, James speaks of "stumbling in one part" (*ptaisē en heni*), with imagery that anticipates the phrase "wander from the truth" in 5:19. Failing in one area is enough to lead one away from God, and those who do this are as condemned as if they had broken all the laws (*pantōn henochos*, literally "answerable for them all"). Certainly murder or apostasy are more serious sins, but economic or racial discrimination is a type of apostasy because it destroys your relationship with God and renders you liable to divine judgment.

So those who discriminate may as well have broken all of God's laws in terms of their standing with God. The courtroom metaphor still continues, and the point is that they will still stand before their heavenly Judge and be sentenced to eternal damnation.

They are guilty of breaking the whole law because it is an indissoluble whole and cannot be separated into isolated parts. They may be completely faithful to the purity laws and the Sabbath rules, but they are still a transgressor and guilty of sin against God and others in the community. So they are judged as unfaithful transgressors.

The reason (*gar*, "for") they are guilty as transgressors is explained in verse 11. James uses two of the Ten Commandments to prove his point. The injunctions against both adultery and murder are the seventh and sixth commandments respectively, stemming from the second table of the Decalogue, the ethical mandates for Israel. You don't have to break both to be a lawbreaker. To be an adulterer but not a murderer still renders you guilty in the eyes of the eternal Judge.

The authority of these commands is not just because Moses wrote them down, but because God himself spoke them. As divine fiats, they are especially important. He probably chose murder as one because prejudice is a destructive force, thus a type of murder. The two are often found together (Matt 5:21, 27; 19:18), and appear together in James 4:2, 4, where murder is linked with slander and conflict in the community and adultery with living for wealth and pleasure. James's emphasis is on the fact that discrimination against the poor is a sin not unlike adultery and murder, as both transgress the law of the one true God, and anyone who transgresses any one of them stands guilty before the one God.

ACT IN LIGHT OF JUDGMENT (2:12–13)

The conclusion for this section goes back to 1:22–25 and the command to turn what you say into actions that determine your lifestyle. This flows out of the three injunctions of 1:19. It is not enough to hear or to speak; you must act on what you hear by both speaking and living out the divine principles in your life. The present-tense imperatives ("Speak and act") indicate that this is to be the ongoing way God's people live. God in his law demands that there be an intimate connection between our thought life (implicit), how we communicate to others, and how we live out his injunctions, especially his command to avoid favoritism. The latter half of this chapter, which is about making certain our faith is expressed in our works (vv. 14–26), will flow out of this command. Speech and action describe the two ways discrimination is shown in the community. Both must be severely curtailed to make certain they serve God rather than sin.

The *houtōs* ("in this way"; not translated in the NIV) at the beginning of verse 12 depicts the need to both speak and act while remembering that you will be "judged by the law that gives freedom." God gave us his laws to liberate us from sin by telling what conduct he expected from us. The "law that gives freedom" stems from 1:25 and refers to the new-covenant teaching of Jesus. The Greek states that we are "about to be judged" (*mellontes krinesthai*), stressing the imminence of the coming judgment. Jesus has freed us from the power of sin, but this new freedom holds us accountable to God to live it out in our daily life.

We must defeat the human tendency to look down on others, especially the poor, and mistreat them. This realization must guide us at all times, for we will "give an account" to God and Christ (Heb 13:17), and we must at all times make certain we reflect the holiness of God, especially the two aspects of that holiness, his justice and love. His love has freed us from sin and death and enables us to love our neighbor. His justice demands that sin be condemned and eradicated from our community.

To anchor the seriousness of this command James turns to **lex talionis**, "the law of retribution," that God will judge us with complete justice on the basis of how we have treated others (2:13). The message is that you won't get away with a thing, for God is omniscient and knows your every thought and action. His justice demands that people be "repaid" for exactly what they have done, reward for the good and judgment for the evil. We are saved by grace, but we will be judged by our works—that is, what we have done to God and others. This is a major doctrine in the Old Testament (2 Chr 6:3; Ps 28:4; Prov 24:12; Ezek 18:20), intertestamental literature (1 Enoch 41:1–2; Psalms of Solomon 2:16–17; 4 Ezra 7:35), and the New Testament (Matt 16:27; Rom 14:12; 2 Cor 5:10; 1 Pet 1:17; Rev 2:23; 22:12).

So when we discriminate against others in any way, "judgment without mercy will be shown to anyone who has not been merciful." We will give account to God and stand before him in shame (2 Tim 2:15; Heb 13:17). We must carefully watch our speech (1:19) and make certain that our actions liberate rather than beat down the poor (1:22–25). God's law demands we love others (2:8) and help rather than hurt the unfortunate. In the Lord's Prayer, forgiveness was the only element on which Jesus added commentary, and the message is a perfect example of the point here as well: if we forgive (or show mercy), we are forgiven (and shown mercy). If we do not forgive or show mercy, we will not be forgiven or shown mercy by God. In fact, this provides the perfect summary for biblical ethics: What we do to others we are actually doing to God (in any area, including discrimination), and he will return those actions back on our heads as either reward or judgment.

To show mercy is literally "to do acts of mercy" (poiēsanti eleos), which better shows James's continuing stress on "doing" (1:22, 23, 25; 2:8, 12). God is a God of mercy (Exod 34:6; Deut 4:31; Neh 9:31; Ps 111:4) and commands his people to be likewise (Hos 6:6; Mic 6:8; Zech 7:9; Matt 18:33; 25:34–45). In fact, the command here is the other side of the beatitude in Matthew 5:7: "Blessed are the merciful, for they will be shown mercy." To be merciless toward the poor is to face a merciless God, and the only way to receive mercy is to show mercy. In this sense favoritism is an act of apostasy, for it will unleash a merciless God of judgment on such perpetrators of sin. Their destiny will be that of the godless.

Still, James ends on a positive note: "Mercy triumphs over judgment." There is debate over whether this mercy is God's or ours. Surely it combines the two. Both sides of the equation are intended here. Our mercy toward the poor must be victorious over our tendency to judge and discriminate against them, and then God will pour out his mercy on us rather than judge us. "Triumphs" is *katakauchatai*, which can also mean "boasts against" or "exults over" (Rom 11:18), but here it means that our mercy must "conquer" our evil disposition toward prejudice and ensue in acts of mercy. We are to emulate God's mercy in our dealings with others, especially the unfortunate and marginalized.

———

This passage (2:1–13) is the second practical demonstration of wisdom in this section (after the need for conduct that is in keeping with our faith in 1:19–27) and introduces the central problem of favoritism for the rich over the poor (2:1–4). This apparently had happened on occasion when wealthy visitors came into the church and the leaders sat them in the most prestigious seats, then forced the poor members of the church to stand in the back or sit on the floor. James castigates such prejudice as judging others against the will of God.

He follows this castigation with four questions that show how inconsistent and wrong the church leaders' actions are (vv. 5–7). First, the poor are special to God and especially favored as heirs of God's blessings. How could they prefer the pagan rich who have only this world and look down on those God has made his special possession? Not only that, but the next three questions show that the rich they prefer are the very ones who are oppressing them and mocking their Lord. Their joining their very enemies and slandering their fellow poor through favoritism is a serious sin and will result in God's judgment of them.

The fact is that we now have the royal law of love (vv. 8–9), the new Torah that has come through King Messiah and is built on God's love for us. This law of love produces in us a special love for one another, so there is no room for prejudice in this new spiritual dynamic. Loving our neighbor means that we care as much for the poor as we do the rich, and to fail to do so is a serious sin that God will have to punish. Moreover, it's not possible to say that you are overcoming one small sin by keeping all the other divine rules, for breaking one law makes you a "lawbreaker," guilty of violating the whole law (vv. 10–11). Showing discrimination is a type of murder, for you are destroying the poor person's reputation and place in the community. It is a great sin to do so.

In the final point of this section (vv. 12–13), James returns to the emphasis on hearing and doing from 1:22–25. The principle is clear—how we think determines how we speak to and treat others, and our speech determines how we act toward them. So it is essential that we "speak and act" on the basis of the realization that we will be judged by the way we treat others. God's laws have been given to liberate people not only from sin but also from being sinned against. When we show favoritism, we are turning against God's liberating laws and heaping judgment on ourselves. Finally, he reminds us that what we do to others God will do to us. We must reject prejudice and show mercy to the poor if we expect God to be merciful toward us.

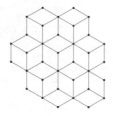

FAITH ACCOMPANIED BY WORKS
(2:14–26)

This section is often labeled the core of the book, since it combines the emphasis on the poor with the need to act on faith commitments, summing up chapter 1. It continues the themes of the last section, demonstrating how works of mercy will prove that the claim to faith is real. As I said in the last section, this is the third of three illustrations showing how wisdom must be put to work in solving the serious problem of trials and poverty in the Christian life, moving from the works that must put into practice the truths we receive from the Lord (1:19–27), to the danger of allowing prejudice to mar the church as it tries to alleviate the struggles of the poor (2:1–13), and now to the necessity of proving our faith by our works (2:14–26). We could say that 2:1–13 addresses the *what* (removing discrimination from the church) and 2:14–26 the *how* (adding works to our faith) of the main ethical problems of the readers. The "works" are the acts of mercy mandated by the law of love in the church.

The challenge develops via three sections: (1) A workless faith is a worthless faith, for when God's people refuse to aid the poor they negate the very salvation they are supposed to proclaim (vv. 14–17). (2) A supporter of James criticizes those who claim faith but remain without works (vv. 18–20). (3) Two Old Testament examples—Abraham (vv. 21–24) and Rahab (vv. 25–26)— demonstrate the inestimable value of a works-oriented faith.

TRUE FAITH IS IMPOSSIBLE
WITHOUT WORKS (2:14–17)

THE KEY QUESTION (2:14)

James states the central issue as a rhetorical question: What profit could there possibly be for anyone to claim they have saving faith when there are no good works to demonstrate its presence? This deep connection between faith and works was a central issue in Judaism as well (4 Ezra 9:7–8, "either by faith or works"). Since for Christians especially faith was seen as the basis of salvation (1:3, 6; 2:1; 5:15), this question is truly at the heart of the entire letter. It is written as a question expecting the answer "no" (= "Is it any good to claim faith but have no deeds? No"). These people may argue that they have a viable faith in Christ, but the absence of good deeds proves they do not.

The question is whether "this type of faith" claimed by these people (*hē pistis*, called an "article of previous reference" as it points back to verse 14a) is still a valid faith. The answer is that it is not. The "if" (*ean*) introduces an element of doubt. Those in the church making such a pretentious claim prove themselves wrong by their favoritism and their failure to help the poor (1:27) with good works. Clearly "faith" is the key word here, and the whole letter has led up to this point. Without a lifestyle centered on good works to bolster what you say, such a boast is worthless. To say you have faith and yet lack works to prove its presence in your life leads to the conclusion that there is actually no faith at all to "save them." In other words, they are not believers, a devastating indictment.

To claim saving faith is not the same as truly having it, and the absence of love and concern for the poor has shown what they say to be false. The kind of faith that would not produce merciful deeds of kindness could never produce eternal life, because it is not true saving faith but mere religious pretense. Two concomitant facts must be brought together, stemming from Ephesians 2:8–10: we are saved by grace, not works (vv. 8–9), yet God has created us for good works (v. 10). Our works don't save us, but they are necessary to show that salvation has truly occurred.

Illustration: Insufficient Food and Clothes (2:15–16)

James supports his point with an illustration about believers who do not have sufficient clothes or food to support themselves. Their dilemma was common in the early church, as seen in the widows of Acts 6:1–6 and the poor who necessitated the collection for the poor (Rom 15:31; 1 Cor 16:1–4; 2 Cor 8–9). Yet here the problem is exacerbated by the kind of false "faith" exhibited in verse 14. The Greek term James uses is literally translated "naked," but it doesn't have to mean that the poor person in question has no clothes at all; it is a euphemism for insufficient clothes and is followed by insufficient food. The "daily food" is likely taken from the Lord's Prayer, "Give us today our daily bread" (Matt 6:11; Luke 11:3). God expects to answer this need through his people as they support the poor in their community.

The so-called faith person responds to the desperate need with a seemingly pious prayer (2:16) that masks a cold heart underneath. "Go in peace" was a normal Jewish farewell (Judg 6:23; 1 Sam 1:17; 2 Kgs 5:19), translated in the NLT as "Good-bye and have a good day." They are sending along best wishes for the journey of life. The added "keep warm and well fed" on the surface was a kind wish — may they find sufficient clothes and food to meet their needs. It seems all well and good.

However, behind the seemingly kind phrases was a refusal to help. They were actually saying, "May God provide you food and clothes because we don't plan to lift a finger to help you." The prayer is actually, "Go away. We hope you find peace, but it won't come from us." When you in reality do "nothing about their physical needs," you have disproved all the seeming good intentions and violated your very claim to be a Christian. In fact, given the corporate nature of Judaism and Christianity, the entire community stands guilty in the eyes of God for allowing such a travesty to occur in the first place. Caring for the needy is not an occasional command to be followed merely whenever you feel like doing so. It is an ongoing mandate that must characterize God's people at all times (Prov 19:17; 21:13; 22:2; Luke 4:18–19; 6:20–26; 16:1–13; 2 Cor 8:9; 1 Tim 6:17–19; 1 John 3:17–18). The end of verse 16 repeats the beginning of verse 15 and forms an **inclusio**—"what good [or 'profit'] is it?" There is no value, and no one who does such a thing has experienced God's salvation.

CONCLUSION: LIFELESS FAITH (2:17)

The conclusion is provided in 2:17 and restates 2:14. Faith that "is not accompanied by action" or works is dead (*nekra*)—not worthless, useless, empty, void, but lifeless, with no future existence. In other words, it was never actually faith in the first place, but now even the claim of faith has been emptied of life. Still, the actual contrast is not between faith and works but between a dead, useless faith without works and a true living faith that must by its very nature produce works. To fail to care for the poor provides a death knell for any pretension of faith. It is not faith and works but faith leading to works that God demands. Without works "faith by itself" is merely a claim without any foundation in reality. It is no more of a real entity than a lifeless corpse is a living person.

This verse is at the center of a well-known debate on James's relationship to Paul. Since Paul stresses that one is saved by grace alone through faith and not by works (Eph 2:8–9), several see a conflict with James's "faith without works is dead." Two reconciliations have been suggested. Many see James trying to correct a distortion of Paul, but I have argued that James is writing in the 40s, slightly before Paul's time, so James would most likely not have been facing any such misreading of Paul.[1] Instead, I would follow those who say James and Paul are looking at two different sides

---

1. See "Provenance and Date" in the introduction.

of the matter. Paul is addressing the issue of regeneration, while James is looking at the Christian life and professing faith. Paul, when speaking of faith, means "saving faith," as a new convert opens her heart to the Spirit and God's salvation. Then by "works" Paul means the works of the law that held salvific value for many Jews. James by "faith" has in mind professing faith of those who are supposedly already Christians, and by "works" means good works exhibited by believers. Paul and James are not in conflict but are each talking of a different issue in the Christian life.

SOMEONE CRITIQUES THE WORKS PEOPLE (2:18-19)

There is significant difference of opinion over the identity of the objector in this passage. The question is whether this interlocutor is opposed to James or to the "faith" people, and also how far his quotation goes. There are two possible interpretations:

1. The interlocutor is a friend of James who is criticizing the man in 2:15-16. So his opening statement is literally intended—"*You* have faith; *I* have deeds." The challenge then flows out of this contrast. The one claiming faith has to prove his faith is genuine but has to do so "without deeds," that is, without any works that prove a true faith lies behind his claims. On the other hand, this friend of James can prove that there is actually a true faith behind his actions because he has good works to back him up ("by my deeds").

2. The interlocutor is an opponent of James. In support of this approach, "but someone will say" in Greek normally introduces an objection to a thesis rather than support. The pronouns "you" and "I" support the first approach, so this view translates them as "one" and "another," thereby allowing the second position to be maintained.

Another question is how much is included in the statement of the interlocutor. The first understanding sees all of verse 18 as the statement of the objector (NASB, KJV). The second view takes only verse 18a as the statement (NIV, NLT, ESV, LEB, NET). By this second approach, verse 18b is James's critique of the faith-only position.

This second interpretation has become the accepted view of nearly all recent scholars, but I have serious reservations. The phrase "but someone will say" does indeed introduce an objector, but the objector is opposing the "faith" people and arguing on the side of James, thus translating in effect, "But someone will say *to you*." This makes much better sense of the pronouns and removes the clumsiness of the second interpretation. This interlocutor is stating that only their and James's understanding is fair to a true claim to faith. The point is that if deeds aren't present, there was never any faith in the first place. This builds on 2:14–17. Without works there is no faith; what they claim is dead and worthless. Their claim is unsupportable when there are no good works to back them up. "Show" means to "make visible for all to see" and provides proof of validity. So the challenge is, "Where is the proof?"

In 2:19 James adds his voice to the interlocutors, pointing to the Shema of Deuteronomy 6:4 (recited thrice daily by Jews), which is central to Christian as well as Jewish belief (also Mark 12:29): "Hear, O Israel: The LORD our God, the LORD is one." They claim faith in God, and James is saying, "Good for you" (the same as "it is good" in 2:8). However, this "good for you" is sarcastic, for there is no "good" when the faith claim fails to be anchored in the works that alone can prove it is valid. Mere assent without substance does no good and proves nothing. They only seem to have a correct theology, but there is nothing to commend it.

The last part of the verse pulls the rug right out from under such shallow claims. By making such an ungrounded claim, they are no better than the demons who "believe that—and shudder." They know without a doubt that there is "one God" and that he is Yahweh, for they were cast out of heaven by this one God and his angels (Rev 12:7–9) and have been engaged in conflict with him ever since. Moreover, their belief ensues in action, for they "shudder" in fear of this one God and never take him for granted. These shallow so-called Christians have no "works," not even that of worship and a healthy fear of failing him.

So they are worse than the demons, who are in reality more orthodox and more monotheistic since they react properly to the reality of the one God. In the Gospels the highest **Christology** comes not out of the mouths of the disciples but from the demonic realm. In Mark 1:24 a demon upon encountering Jesus blurts out, "I know who you are—the Holy One of God"; in 3:11 the demons shriek, "You are the Son of God"; and in 5:7 one screams, "What do you want with me, Jesus, Son of the Most High God?" They realize who he is and quake with fear, knowing the certainty of the judgment awaiting them. These foolish "faith" people should feel the same terror as the demons, for in reality they stand indicted by God and are under judgment for their lack of good works.

This is stated clearly in Revelation 12:12: "But woe to the earth and the sea, because the devil has gone down to you! He is filled with fury, because he knows that his time is short." Their assent is based on certain knowledge of their destined end, which lies in absolute contrast with the smug complacency of these "faith" people, who fail to be "slow to speech" (1:19) and to act on what they claim to believe (1:22–25). The demons are the implacable enemies of God and "shudder" with the reality this produces. The "faith" people are also headed for judgment but remain unaware of their plight because of their shallow confession of faith.

JAMES ILLUSTRATES FROM THE OLD TESTAMENT (2:20–26)

THE BASIC TRUTH (2:20)

The rhetorical question of 2:20—"do you want evidence that faith without deeds is useless?"—restates 2:17 and is a transition passage, both concluding verses 18–19 and introducing 21–26. In other words, it sums up what has been said and prepares for what is coming. This section is in the form of a "diatribe," a challenge to opponents in a debate. These "foolish" or "empty-headed" people have still failed to realize the central truth behind it all, that "faith without deeds is useless." Their problem is that by an act of the will they have refused to "recognize" or "realize" (*gnōnai*) the actual truth about the validity of their faith stance. In other words, they know this but refuse to face it. Thus they are "fools" not just in an intellectual sense but in a moral sense.

What they refuse to face is the central theme of this section (2:14–16), that any claim to faith without works to prove it is "useless" and "empty." The passage escalates throughout—faith apart from works has no "good" value or profit (v. 14), then it is "dead" (v. 17), and now it is "useless." The Greek term for this is *argē*, with the *a*-privative (negating an idea) and *ergon* (work), meaning "without work" or "unproductive, ineffective, useless" (used in Matt 20:3, 6 of idle workers). You could say such faith is "worthless" because it is "workless." Such people refuse to work at their faith and so prove it isn't there in the first place.

FAITH AND WORKS WITH ABRAHAM (2:21–24)

To prove his premises regarding faith and works, James uses two key Old Testament examples, moving from logical arguments to historical and scriptural ones—namely, Abraham and Rahab. As the father of the nation, Abraham is the natural place to begin. He is called "father" in several places (Isa 51:2; Matt 3:9; Rom 4:1, 11–12, 17). The Jewish people have their self-identity in being "Abraham's children" (John 8:39), and through him they were the covenant people (Luke 19:9; Acts 13:26). So there was a strong precedent for Abraham as the archetypal Jew and model of the pious Israelite.

With another question expecting a yes answer (2:5, 6, 7, 14, 18, 20), James brings out their memory of Abraham as the model "righteous" person. The verb he uses is *dikaioō*, the verb for "being justified" by faith alone in Romans 3:24; 4:25; 8:30; 1 Corinthians 6:11; Galatians 2:16–17; 3:6. Some see a contradiction since this comes close to "justified by works" while Paul declares "not by works" in Ephesians 2:9 (also Rom 3:28; 4:2, 4–6). However, this is not the case, as we discussed earlier at 2:17. James and Paul are not antithetical regarding faith and works. They are using *dikaioō* in different ways, Paul emphasizing the forensic side, the declaration of legal justification (the judicial aspect) that takes place at conversion when God declares us to be right with him.

James is using the verb in its ethical sense (righteous living) as part of living for God after conversion. Abraham's act of offering "his son Isaac on the altar" proved he was a "righteous" person, and some would translate this as "vindicated by his act." Abraham's faith had led him to be "counted as righteous" in Genesis 15:6, and then in Genesis 22 God tested his faith (a faith already present in him) in the incident called "the binding of Isaac" (called the Akedah, or "binding"), seen by the Jews as the example par excellence of his moral obedience and righteousness before God (1 Maccabees 2:52; Sirach 44:20; Wisdom 10:5). Abraham's faith had to be proved by his deeds, and it was.

In verse 22 James explains his point about Abraham further. With "you see" James directly addresses the faith person from 2:14–16 to make certain he realizes that Abraham's "faith and his actions were working together." The Greek here is a wordplay, "faith working with his works," emphasizing the point that neither faith nor works can operate apart from each other. When isolated from one another they cease to exist, becoming either a false claim (faith alone) or a self-centered work (deeds alone). They must be coworkers on the walk of life to be true. Genesis 15:6 (faith and righteousness) had to be put into action in Genesis 22 (faith and works), lest the former become unreal and false, both unrealized and unverifiable.

The truth is that Abraham's faith was "made complete," or "perfect" (*eteleiōthē*), recalling 1:4, where James mandated that "perseverance" be allowed to "finish" its work so that we might become "mature and complete." The two aspects of our Christian walk, our faith and our actions, must be allowed to bring each other to maturity and complete God's work in us. The truth is that our faith can only attain its God-intended goal when we act on it via good deeds. The emphasis is on the fact that Abraham's faith empowered him to do his works and then guided his works, with the two working together to make him a mature follower of God. Note the progression: faith leads to our works, the two work together in our lives, the two bring our relationship to God to completion, and we are made whole and complete as believers.

In this process "the scripture was fulfilled" (2:23) regarding Abraham. To "fulfill" means to "fill to the full." The passage James has in mind is Genesis 15:6, cited here as "Abraham believed God, and it was credited to him as righteousness." This process by which he was "credited ... as righteous" was not complete until he acted on it in Genesis 22. There are two results of the partnership of faith and works in Abraham: the fulfillment or completion of the process in his being "credited" as righteous (Gen 15:6), and the fact that he is called "God's friend" (see also 2 Chr 20:7; Isa 41:8).

The first is the famous "imputation of righteousness" passage Paul cites in Romans 4:3, and James is adding that the binding of Isaac completed that faith decision as he acted on his faith and brought it to maturity. There were two stages by which this took place. God "credited" or "reckoned" that faith to be a sign of Abraham's righteousness (Gen 15:6), and then when he put that faith into action at the binding of Isaac (Gen 22) he took it to a new level, demonstrating and proving the reality of God's declaration in Genesis 15.

As a result of this maturation of Abraham's righteousness, he "was called God's friend," probably a divine passive meaning "God called him his friend." Several passages highlight this. In Genesis 18:17, when Abraham interceded for Sodom, God showed his intimate trust and acceptance of him when he said, "Shall I hide from Abraham what I am about to do?" The Jewish philosopher Philo interpreted this as, "Shall I hide this from Abraham my friend?" (*Sobriety* 56). He is frequently called God's friend in other Jewish writings (Jubilees 19:9; Testament of Abraham 1:6; 2:3; 4 Ezra 3:14). In 2 Chronicles 20:7 and Isaiah 41:8 he is called the friend of God. In this there is a contrast between Abraham and those who like him prove their faith by their deeds, as opposed to those whose "friendship with the world" makes them an "enemy of God" (Jas 4:4).

James concludes in 2:24, "You see that a person is considered righteous by what they do and not by faith alone." James has said this now four times (with 2:14, 17, 20), so it is the central point of the section. This time James has moved "by works" to the beginning of the verse to stress its importance as the key point. Faith becomes true faith only when it is shown to be real on the basis of the good deeds it produces. It is "by what they do" that what they believe is proved valid. The three main points are shown in relationship to one another. People, when they are converted to Christ, are *justified* on the basis of a *faith* that is made real by their *works*.

Interestingly, the slogan "by faith alone" is not found in Paul and only here in James. So James recognizes the place of faith in the Christian life and is simply stressing that it does not function "alone." Unless it ensues in good works, it is "dead" and "useless." Paul actually agrees with James on the important place of good deeds in the Christian walk (1 Cor 3:10–15; 2 Cor 9:8; Gal 6:4; Eph 2:10; Col 1:10; 1 Tim 2:10; 5:25; 6:18). As discussed in 2:12 the doctrine of "judged by the law" fits well with James here and is found throughout Scripture. James agrees that the doctrine of justification includes the final verdict of God when we give account of our lives and work at the final judgment. Putting Paul and James together, it would read: "You are saved by grace through faith, not by works (for instance, the works of the law); but once you are saved, you must prove it by good works, and at the last judgment, you will be judged (receive reward or judgment) on the basis of the works you have done."

FAITH AND WORKS WITH RAHAB (2:25–26)

"In the same way" means that James is adding a second example after Abraham that proves his principle that faith must be "justified" and the claimant "shown to be righteous" (*edikaiōthē*) by the good works of the individual.[2] However, Rahab is quite a different example, being a female, undoubtedly poor, and a prostitute who had thus far lived an immoral life. This is a very important addition, for it shows that what James is saying applies to everyone, and that God can use anyone for his purposes. Forgiveness is available to all.

Rahab's story takes place in Joshua 2, where she saved the two Israelite spies in Jericho. She did two things—"gave lodging to the spies" and hid them in her home (possibly a tavern or brothel). This was part of the town wall, and so she lowered them by a rope down the wall and "sent them off in a different direction," thereby saving them from the Jericho militia. As a result she became one of the "heroes" of Jewish tradition and was known as a model of hospitality.[3] Both were considered archetypal converts to the worship of the true God, Abraham from Ur and Rahab from Jericho. The message here of course is that she was "shown to be righteous" by her actions, and was even included as part of the messianic line to Jesus according to Matthew 1:5.

Though a pagan, a citizen of Jericho, and a prostitute, she confessed her faith in Joshua 2:11, saying "the LORD your God is God in heaven above and on the earth below." Then she acted on her faith and hid the messengers, saving them from the soldiers. As a result

---

2. As I stated in my comments on 2:17, 21, the thrust of both "faith" and "justified" in James does not contradict Paul. James is stating that while a person is saved by faith, he is "shown to be justified" by his works, meaning his true faith is both proved in this present world and vindicated at the last judgment.

3. She has been celebrated down through the centuries in Jewish writings like b. Megillah 14b–15a; Exodus Rabbah 27:4.

she became considered a model of faith in the New Testament (Heb 11:31) and other early Christian writings (1 Clement 10–12). Here she is also a model of faith-based works.

For the fifth and final time (with 2:14, 17, 20, 24) James highlights the thesis of this section: "Faith without deeds is dead." He uses a powerful analogy to make his point. Faith without works is just as dead as "the body without the spirit," nothing but a lifeless hunk of flesh. So good works are the life force of any claim to faith. It is not just that faith is brought to life by these deeds; without them there was no faith at all from the very start. Such a faith hasn't died. It had never ever been alive. It was a corpse and had at all times been a corpse. In Genesis 2:7 God "breathed ... the breath of life" into Adam and he became "a living being." James is saying that in the same way good deeds "breathe life" into faith. Any faith that is not animated by works is no faith at all.

––––––

Here we are at the heart of the problem. These Jewish Christians in James's churches are claiming to have faith, but all the problems he has already addressed show that they are not backing up their faith claim with the deeds that show it to be a valid claim (vv. 14–17). Their failure to obey the injunctions of the new Torah of the Messiah, the "law" Jesus has taught them (1:22–25) and the discrimination they have shown the poor in their congregations in favor of rich visitors (2:1–13), tends to put the lie to the claim to faith. When they fail to help the poor, their very walk with Christ comes into question (vv. 15–16). Clearly, the so-called faith of such a person is lifeless, with no evidence to support the validity of such a claim (v. 17). This point is as real today as it was in James's day. We must care for the needy if our claim to faith is to hold up as real.

So James turns to a supporter and lodges his devastating criticism of the "faith" people (vv. 18–19). They have a verbal faith claim but nothing to back it up, no evidence to show it is real faith. He and James, on the other hand, have works that prove the faith they have to be true faith. While many today doubt this understanding, the use of pronouns here favors it, for it is clumsy to retranslate "you" and "I" as "one" and "another." So this person is a friend of James and an opponent of the "faith" people.

In verse 19 James adds his voice to that of the objector and calls for these shallow faith-without-works people to join the demons who unlike them understand the reality of the Shema (there is one God) and "shudder." They realize it means eternal judgment, while these shallow faith-only individuals blithely go their way without recognizing the seriousness of their plight—namely, that judgment is coming.

The rest of this section turns to two "heroes of the faith," Abraham and Rahab, to prove the reality of this claim. It begins with the thesis of the whole section (v. 20), that faith unaccompanied by deeds is workless and worthless. There is no truth whatsoever to such claims, for they produce nothing of value and thus are under condemnation from God.

Abraham is the archetypal example (vv. 21–24), for "his faith was made complete by what he did" when he bound his promised son, Isaac, and put him on the altar to sacrifice him to God in Genesis 22, stated in Genesis 15:6 to be the act "credited as righteousness" by God. Abraham's work proved his faith and was seen as a righteous deed by God, demonstrating this as God's will for his people (and thus for us as well). Faith must lead to works to be efficacious. The result is twofold: Abraham became God's "friend," and his works led him to be labeled righteous in God's sight.

Rahab (vv. 25–26) exemplifies the same principle. As a prostitute in Jericho, she believed in the God of the Jews but added works when she hid the spies and secreted them out of the city, saving their lives (Josh 2). So she put her faith to work and showed it was real. The result is she became a hero and a model of faith shown in works forevermore.

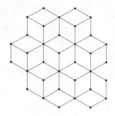

THE DANGER OF THE TONGUE
(3:1–12)

At first glance the section begun by these verses, on the danger of the tongue and the need to gain control over it (3:1–4:12), seems isolated and independent from what we have seen thus far. This would support the theory that James is an artificial collection of wisdom essays thrown together haphazardly. However, a closer look shows that it is closely related to the rest of the material and is the third and final example of practical Christianity flowing out of chapter 1, after the problems of prejudice (2:1–13) and faith without works (2:14–26). The need for wisdom (1:5–8) to combat a failed Christian ethic is proved in these three examples.

In this section James is developing further his mandates to avoid improper speech (1:19, 22–25). At the same time, he expands this greatly and turns it into the next major part of his essay (3:1–4:12) with an ABA pattern: A: Taming the tongue (3:1–12); B: The need for wisdom in our speech (3:13–18); A': The tongue causing conflict (4:1–12). In this approach, the A sections identify the negative problem; the B section, the positive solution. This is an incredibly practical section, similar to parts of Proverbs, and deserves to be one of the first sermon series or Bible studies at the beginning of any new ministry. There is not one of us who doesn't fight the problem of the tongue. Big mouths and flippant tongues have destroyed all too many lives.

BEWARE OF BECOMING
TEACHERS (3:1-2A)

Whenever James is going to challenge his readers, he lets them know he considers them "brothers and sisters" (1:2, 9, 16, 19; 2:1, 5, 14, 15; NIV: "my fellow believers") to show them he loves them and considers them family under the Lord. Probably because teachers in the first century were so highly regarded, many in the community were aspiring to that role in order to be viewed and treated as leaders. In the **Hellenistic** world it was the pedagogue; in the Jewish world, the rabbi. Jesus was called "rabbi" (Mark 9:5; John 1:38) or "teacher" (Matt 8:19; 12:38; Mark 5:35; 9:17, 38; Luke 7:40; 11:45; John 20:16). The scribes were "teachers of the law" and received their status from the fact that they guarded Torah truth and disseminated it to the people. In the church it was the elder-pastors who were the teachers, and they were the rabbis of the Christian community. All three terms—teacher, elder, pastor—stood for the same office in the early church.

So this became the highest office there was under that of the apostles (Acts 13:1; 1 Cor 12:28; Eph 4:11). The problem was that many of those who wanted the office were immature believers and not ready for so public a role. The teachers had to know the word, become its guardians in light of the false teachers sneaking into the church, and teach it regularly to the people. These shallow seekers of power and attention were not ready for such a role. Too often this teaching led to bickering, dissension, and struggles for power and prestige (1 Cor 10:10; Phil 2:3-4, 14; 1 Pet 3:9; Jude 16). Diotrophes in 3 John 9-10 is a "perfect" example, one who "loved to be first" and spread "malicious" lies about John and the other true leaders. So as today those with important ministries also were more accountable to God. Their high role carried with it great responsibility to fulfill that role. So he tells them, "Not many of you should become teachers." The teaching office in the church is a calling, not a position to be casually sought in order to gain status in the community. It should never be sought for the glory of it and for the influence it gave one over the church. God alone is to choose who holds the position.

So they are warned about the reason to be cautious: "because you know that we who teach will be judged more strictly." James is not arguing against the office but warning of the dangers. He includes himself ("we") to show this applied to all leaders. There are four levels to the "judgment" intended here: (1) The public use of the tongue exposed them to serious temptation (1:12–15), and that could result in judgment. (2) Since Christian teachers hold this high office, they have all the greater responsibility before God and the church to use it wisely. (3) Those teachers misusing their tongues and damaging the church would face greater condemnation. (4) The judgment would take place both on the earthly plane (as the church recognized their failures and acted) and on the heavenly plane (at the final judgment).

In the latter sense, they would "give an account" to God (Heb 13:17), and those who have failed will stand in shame at the throne of judgment (2 Tim 2:15). James means it both ways, as those who exercise the office well will receive great reward and those who fail will face great reprobation. This is a warning we all today should treat very seriously. There is simply way too much shallow ministry taking place in all too many churches! The quality of one's leadership, teaching, and preaching matters a great deal to God as well as the church, and so we must be careful with what we say and when we say it.

The rest of this section will develop and apply this basic principle not just to the leaders but to all believers, and James begins that wider application in verse 2a when he says, "We all stumble in many ways." No one is perfect (1 John 1:8, 10), and all of us are fallible, including our teachers. Every one of us makes mistakes. *Ptaiō* means literally to "trip," here to "trip up" as a result of our many errors, especially here the sins of speech that hurt our ministry. "Many ways" means that our mistakes are not just many in number but different in types of errors of speech. Our goal must be to continue to mature and cut down on these sins, but it is also to recognize when we are not ready for leadership and to wait until we are ready.

A SMALL THING HAS GREAT RESULTS (3:2B–5A)

THE GOAL: CONTROLLING THE TONGUE (3:2B)

The truth is, James goes on to say, a person who always controlled their tongue would be "perfect," a sinless person, for that would mean they are "able to keep their whole body in check." None of us have attained that, but it is a fact (he uses a "condition of fact," *ei*, to make his point) that this would be the case. It is the goal for which we all strive, and in a sense all of 3:1–4:12 is intended to enable us to work toward this end, to learn to control our tongues and avoid the "faults" and mistakes in what we say that can cause so much damage. Notice too that he does not have in mind just the leaders of the church but all true believers. All of us fit into this category and must start using our tongue to glorify God and not just serve ourselves. Many teachers use their speaking skills to gain control of churches, but they have forgotten that they need to gain control over their tongues before they try to take over churches.

"Perfect" here goes beyond 1:4, where it refers to the "mature and complete" Christian to point to sinless perfection. His point is that if you can completely control the tongue, you can control the whole body and every part of yourself, and thus can attain perfection in this life. The attainment of this perfection will come in our heavenly life to come, but we strive for it in the here and now. The importance of controlling the tongue is a major theme in Proverbs (9:8–9; 10:8, 14, 19; 11:9; 12:18; 13:13; 15:1; 16:21; 17:7; 18:6–7; 21:23). As one who has been a pastor and teacher my entire adult life, I recognize how badly we need to develop in this area, and at the age of seventy-five I am still striving to grow in this. Letting my big mouth roam free has caused me innumerable difficulties throughout my life.

"Keep their whole body in check" is both physical (control our bodily parts) and spiritual (keep us from sin). The point is that what it takes to control the tongue would be sufficient to gain control of every area of our lives. What we say proceeds from how we think and determines how we act, so every area of our life is affected by gaining power over our tongues. Many think "body" here can be extended to the church as the "body" of Christ, and this double meaning is quite viable. If we can control our tongues, the church as well will be under Christ's control and "held in check."

ILLUSTRATING THE POWER OF THE TONGUE (3:3–5A)

Since the tongue is so small a member of the body, it would be possible to consider it of little importance. This would be a disastrous mistake, and James uses four examples to illustrate how much power small things can contain: a bit in a horse's mouth (v. 3), a rudder on a ship (v. 4), the tongue (v. 5a), and a forest fire (v. 5b). These were common examples used by ancient philosophers or writers to illustrate the power of small things like tongues (see Philo, *Allegorical Illustrations* 3.224; Plutarch, *Concerning Talkativeness* 10). The first, the bridle of a horse and small bit placed in the horse's mouth to direct where it goes, is a perfect illustration because of the awe the general populace held for the Roman cavalry and the huge, powerful war horses that were considered invincible in battle. They controlled the tide of every battle, yet the teeny little bits in their mouths allowed the cavalrymen to direct them everywhere they went.

It is disputed whether the "mouths of horses" are meant to parallel the teaching office of the church, and "turn the whole animal" meant to parallel how the teaching determines the direction of the church (NIV's "whole animal" in the Greek is "whole body"). While the application to the body of the church can be disputed, the application to the tongue directing each of our lives is definitely present here. The latter is distinctly intended while the former is a possible further extension. Teachers maintain their leadership on the basis of how effective what they say is in the church, and like a bit with horses they use it to guide the direction a church takes.

The second example is the small rudder on a large ship (3:4). The Romans had learned to build immense ships like the trireme that were so large they had to be propelled by three banks of oars. The massive grain ships (Paul took one to Rome in Acts 27) regularly brought tons of grain from Egypt. Of course, they were not that large compared to our day of aircraft carriers and massive cruise ships, but for the ancient world they were unimaginably huge.

The point is the same: small rudders at the end of the boat controlled completely what direction they took. Here the large-small discrepancy is highlighted to prepare for the tongue in the next verse. He also stresses the "strong winds" that drive the boat and that without the rudder could force it out of control (see Acts 27:14-20). So the rudder takes over for both dangers—the large ship and the strong winds. Without it everything would fall apart. The elements are present in the two illustrations—the large entity that needs control, the small thing that ends up providing that control, and the will of the person who wields that control. James's message is that we must learn to control what we say, for it often determines whether a church is a great success or a massive failure.

The third example is the tongue itself, the main point (3:5a). Here his point becomes explicit: "Likewise, the tongue is a small part of the body, but it makes great boasts." The tongue is virtually the smallest part of the body but in many ways has the greatest effect of any other bodily element. The reason for the negative "great boasts" is because James is stressing in this first section the terrible consequences of the misuse of the tongue. James develops the potential devastating results in verse 6. Some think, however, that it is more neutral here to prepare for the whole section and may be translated, "what great things it can boast about." The neutral sense is probably best, for it is meant to prepare for everything that follows, the good and bad effects the tongue can produce.

The fourth and final illustration is "Consider what a great forest is set on fire by a small spark." Now we turn to the *destructive* potential of small things. It is interesting that for rhetorical effect the same Greek term (*hēlikon*) means both "great" and "small" here. This makes even more stark the image of a "small" spark causing such a "huge" territory to burn down. The Greek word translated "forest" here is "wood" (*hylēn*), and it is possible that the idea is a brushfire: once started, it is almost impossible to stop. All of us, especially if we live in the American Southwest, can identify with the massive destruction a small campfire or even a cigarette can do to thousands of acres of brush or woodland. I find myself aghast at how often a new conflagration breaks out and within a couple weeks consumes enough territory to destroy a small state. And it seems the amount of territory keeps getting greater each year. This is truly a terrifying metaphor!

THE TONGUE HAS DESTRUCTIVE POWER (3:5B–10)

The rest of this paragraph develops the evil power of the tongue to act contrary to God's way and utilize its destructive power. There are three parts: It resembles a small flame that destroys acre after acre (vv. 5b–6); it is incredibly difficult to tame (vv. 7–8); and it is antithetical to God's creation in that it blesses and curses at the same time (vv. 9–12). The three images in verses 3–5 detail the positive effects of the tongue, while the three in verses 6–12 detail its evil effects.

A TERRIBLE POWER TO DESTROY (3:5B–6)

James builds this progressive series of five destructive images on verse 5b, identifying the tongue as a devastating fire, a common metaphor (Pss 10:7; 39:1–3; Prov 16:27; 26:21; Isa 30:27). This brings out the negative side of "makes great boasts" (3:5). It is a descending series (v. 6) that seems to build in intensity with each addition. The idea of the tongue as a fire is especially apropos, as I said in verse 5, for those of us who watch the unbelievable devastation each year from the wildfires in the western United States. As I watch the millions of acres of forest burning down, I recall Revelation 8:7, in which John says that "a third of the earth was burned up, a third of the trees were burned up, and all the green grass was burned up" at the **eschaton** (however we interpret this). This is a powerful image to initiate this series.

Next, it is "a world of evil among the parts of the body." This is a very difficult clause to understand. The Greek literally says "a world of unrighteousness appointing itself among our [bodily] members." There are several things to debate here. Is the genitive "of unrighteousness/evil" a descriptive genitive ("evil world"), objective ("a world producing evil"), or partitive ("the sum total of evil")? Of these, I prefer the descriptive, for it is telling what the tongue has made this world to be—that is, a fallen world filled with evil.

Next, is this picture mainly individual (each of us as depraved) or corporate (centering on the community as corrupt)? The individual sense is the more likely: the tongue disrupts each of us and "represents the world of wrongdoing among the parts of our bodies" (NET). Still, it may well encompass both the personal and the corporate side here, for the tongue enables sin to gain power over us individually and then to use us to wreak havoc in the church community as a whole. These are difficult times, and it seems almost a weekly tragedy that somewhere a pastor has fallen into moral sin or developed a personality cult that tells the world Satan has won yet another skirmish.

Finally, is "appoints" a passive (God makes it what it is)? That would be a difficult choice because it would virtually picture God creating the tongue to be evil. It is much better to see the verb as a middle voice, with the tongue "appointing itself" to be an unrighteous member in our body. This would fit well the idea of the tongue as an act of the will choosing to do evil in our lives. Putting all of this together, the tongue "appoints itself to represent the evil world among the parts of each of our bodies." In the same way that Adam chose to sin and all of us are both born in sin and choose to commit sins (Rom 5:12), our tongues willfully choose to become tools of wickedness.

The third image, then, depicts the tongue as that evil member in us that "corrupts the whole body." Again, this is individual and corporate, for as a person and as the body of Christ we are stained by the effects of the tongue moving into this evil world. This image functions physically as well as spiritually, for angry words cause our stomach acid to boil and our church community to be defiled. The main stress, of course, is on the spiritual results. "Corrupts" brings in the Old Testament thrust of the person "defiled" or "stained," becoming impure before God. The cognate verb is used in 1:27, where we are to keep ourselves "from being polluted by the world." The tongue stains our lives and makes us unworthy of standing in God's presence.

Fourth, evil speech "sets the whole course of one's life on fire." This is even more comprehensive an image, for virtually the whole cycle of our existence is meant, using the birth metaphor and the idea of the wheels of life to picture a blaze spreading wider and wider into a conflagration that wipes out everything. The blaze begins at the center of life and sets on fire the whole cycle of life. It refers to the "ups and downs of life," as the tongue forces a downward spiral on the process that leads the vicissitudes of life to destroy us, while God's purpose is for us to turn to him so he can use these same forces to strengthen us and teach us perseverance (1:2–8). We have a choice to make, to give our tongues free rein and allow the corruption process to proceed all the way in our lives, or to gain control over it and surrender it to God. When we give our tongue over to evil, it consumes us and wipes out everything we are and will ever be.

Fifth and finally, the tongue "is itself set on fire by hell," forming an **inclusio** with the beginning description of it as "a fire" at the start of the verse. The fire is set by Satan (Matt 5:22) as opposed to the purifying fire of the Holy Spirit (Matt 3:11; Acts 2:1–4) or the live coals of God (Isa 6:6–7). "Hell" is "Gehenna" (*geenna*), a reference to the Valley of Hinnom outside the walls of Jerusalem, where the trash fires burned 24/7. It was a place of horror where children had been sacrificed to the pagan god Molech (2 Kgs 23:10; 2 Chr 28:3; Jer 32:35) and by the first century had became a symbol of condemnation. It could be used here to state that Satan takes control of the tongue, but I prefer with many recent scholars to see this describing the punishment for the evil more than its origins, thereby meaning that it has become a fire and therefore a fitting end in the fiery pits of hell.

The Difficulty of Taming It (3:7–8)

In a sense these verses are a further metaphor describing the tongue as a wild, untamable animal. James uses oriental hyperbole to exaggerate how virtually every kind of "animals, birds, reptiles and sea creatures are being tamed and have been tamed by mankind." This looks to Genesis 1:26–28, where God gave humankind dominion over the animal world, and the division here reflects the Genesis 1 division of wildlife. The Romans had tamed lions and tigers, and Hannibal had used elephants in his army. Today we would extend this even to killer whales and many sea creatures unimaginable in James's day. Still, his point is well taken.

The whole of the animal realm is under our control, but not the tongue (3:8). It is as wild as ever, in fact wilder than any animal and even more vicious than the predators. They simply follow nature and the way they were created. The tongue, on the other hand, is personified as "a restless evil, full of deadly poison" and had of its own free will chosen ("made itself," v. 6) to be that way. It is completely out of control, and there is no hope of any ever taming it. However, James actually says "no one *among men*" (*anthrōpōn*), implying that God can do so. As in Mark 10:27, "With man this is impossible, but not with God." Once again, we must turn to the Triune Godhead to find the victory. With Christ, we are "more than conquerors" (Rom 8:37); without him we are doomed to defeat.

The key is our need for the Spirit to take over and empower us to defeat Satan in our lives.

The reason this is so is because of the true nature of the tongue. It is "a restless evil," a strong description meaning more than the tongue's instability (like waves, 1:8) but connoting its uncontrollable power and nature. The tongue always moves toward the wickedness that it has chosen for itself, and we have to fight constantly to gain some semblance of control (Eph 4:39; 5:4), for it is never at rest. Moreover, in its restlessness it is at all times "full of deadly poison." It doesn't just unsettle you, it kills you. In the earthly realm the tongue savors life-giving, nourishing food and avoids what can poison you. In the spiritual realm it does the opposite and destroys both person and community. As in Psalm 140:3, "the poison of vipers is on their lips," a perfect picture, as the sack of poison on a viper is in a little pocket under its mouth (see also Rom 3:13).

THE TWO USES FOR IT (3:9–10)

The tongue is not only powerful in its evil; it is hypocritical. The tongue exhibits the same duplicity as the "double-minded" person of 1:8 who is constantly shifting from the things of God to the things of the world. One moment the mouth is used to praise and worship God; the next it is cursing and slandering those who "have been made in God's likeness." So the "restless evil" is simply a part of the unstable wave-runner (see 1:6–7) that constitutes every human being. James's use of *eulogeō* (bless) makes real sense, for it provides the basic description of worship in Judaism. From time immemorial, whenever Jewish people named God, they would add, "Blessed be he" (Pss 28:6; 31:21; 103:1–2; Rom 9:5; 2 Cor 1:3; 1 Pet 1:3). The double title "Lord and Father" is only here in all the Bible, but the names appear in the same context often (Isa 63:16; 64:8; Matt 11:25; 1 Cor 8:6). So this is highly liturgical here, and it is incredibly comforting. Our powerful Lord of creation is also our loving Father. He always seeks what is best for us and has the power to accomplish exactly that. The only question is whether we will relinquish control to him and allow him to take over our lives.

Yet the next instant, the same mouth, as soon as the worship is over, begins sniping and slandering others in the community. "Curse" was almost a semitechnical phrase used in public forums to call down curses on another person. Here it is used less formally to describe backbiting and bickering as in internecine church battles (4:1-2, 11-12). God poured out covenant blessings on the faithful, while they all too often poured out invective on each other. The saints are supposed to return blessings when cursed (1 Pet 3:9), but too many times they themselves are the source of the curses.

The sad thing is that the very people being cursed have been "made in God's likeness" ("in the image of God"), from Genesis 1:26, "Let us make mankind in our image, in our likeness." To be created in God's image is to be in union with him, and what is done to these people is actually done to God. So when they curse these people, they are actually cursing the very God they had just worshipped. Such duplicity cannot be tolerated and must bring judgment in its wake.

This in fact is how James summarizes the problem in verse 10. The same person should never praise God with one breath and curse people with another. Such hypocrisy should never be. Your speech reflects what you are thinking and who you are. Evil speech comes from an evil heart, and the tongue is the mouthpiece of the heart. It is the mark of a double-minded, wishy-washy person (see Matt 12:33-37; 15:11, 18). So he strongly denounces such duplicitous speech: "My brothers and sisters, this should not be."

JAMES GIVES EXAMPLES OF INCONSISTENCY (3:11-12)

Three illustrations from nature draw this section to a proper conclusion in order to show how illogical and incompatible doubletalk is in the divine order of things. These are all rhetorical questions expecting the answer "no," as in 2:4-5. It is abnormal and against the purposes of God's creation for the tongue to produce good and evil at the same time. The first can be translated, "Fresh water and salt water cannot flow from the same spring, can they?" Springs were at the heart of Palestinian life and were the basis of survival. An area was judged livable on the basis of its access to a freshwater spring (*glyky*, from which we derive "glucose"). Springs don't produce fresh water one day and salt water the next.

This is a vivid metaphor, stemming from a comparison of the Jordan and the Dead Sea, which demonstrated one of the dangers, the infusion of salt water into a fresh spring. A fish swimming down the Jordan toward the Dead Sea would die the second it hit the mineral-laden waters. This could also be alluding to the miracle of Marah (Exod 15:23), when the bitter (the meaning of "Marah") water was turned sweet and drinkable, saving the Israelites in the Desert of Shur (Exod 15:22–25). So the point is that in the same way a spring cannot "gush forth" or "bubble up" (*bryei*) fresh and salty water at the same time, our speech should not pour out blessings and curses. There were no spigots for hot and cold running water back then, and neither did God make the tongue to be that kind of faucet.

The second illustration (3:12a) considers the problem from another perspective—namely, the kind of person you are, which determines the kinds of things you will say to others. It stems from God's created order (Gen 1:11–12), which always remains true to itself. Olives and figs were the two major agricultural products of Palestine. The analogy here is that the fruit will follow the seed or root, and a fig tree will never produce olives or a grapevine bear figs. The fruit will flow out of the kind of tree that produces it. Nature will never turn against itself, and this is the case also with the apex of God's creation, human beings and their tongues. This was a stock source of material for ancient speakers, and Jesus used it of true and false prophets in Matthew 7:16. Only an evil heart will produce a tongue that utilizes speech to hurt others; a good heart will never do so.

The final illustration (3:12b) is another example of the previous point. This time it is a "salt spring"—namely, one that draws its water from the Mediterranean. Such a spring could never bring forth fresh water, for its source would not allow it to do so. James's message is that the type of speech you utter is a barometer of the kind of person you are. Thus you will never be able to control your tongue until you change your heart. An inconsistent, duplicitous tongue means a double-minded person. God did not create you to use your divinely given gift of speech to hurt others. Such sad practices proceed from an evil heart, and so you must begin by repenting and getting right with God. So long as you have an evil heart, you cannot change your evil habits and your terrible results.

———

This issue is so important that James makes it the longest section of the book (3:1–4:12), for the misuse of the tongue has caused so many problems in the Christian community and hurt so many people. It is a danger that has never ceased throughout history and is just as problematic today as it has ever been. In fact, it is far worse since technology like the computer and social media have made it so much easier to slander others. It can destroy individual ministries and whole churches. In 3:1–12 James addresses one of the primary offices, that of teacher, warning that people would be better off not seeking the office, since it carries the greatest responsibility and its misuse affects so many people and thus incurs the greater judgment.

Teachers (vv. 1–2a) have the highest responsibility of anyone since they determine how the church lives out its calling from God. They will be "judged more strictly," meaning they have the greater responsibility to lead the church wisely and make a greater effect on its life as God's people. None of us are perfect; we all make mistakes. Nevertheless, we are responsible to rely on God for strength and trust the Spirit to empower us so we can lead our people as deeply into the truths of God and as carefully into the depths of the word of God as we can. So we desperately need to gain control of our tongues and use the gift of speech to glorify God and hasten the life of the church. In the rest of this section we will learn both negative and positive formulas for doing just that.

The tongue is one of the smallest parts of our body, so James provides four examples (the tongue is third) to illustrate the great effects small things can have (vv. 3–5). The war horse was one of God's most magnificent creatures and could not be stopped in battle, yet it was directed wherever the rider wished by a very small bit in the horse's mouth. Similarly, massive ships like triremes and grain ships were directed by a small rudder in the stern. Finally, a small spark could cause a forest or brushfire that would consume thousands of acres. The tongue too was a spark that could destroy whole communities. We have certainly seen that in the church today. Many church splits are caused not by false doctrine but personality conflicts that get out of hand.

The first step in the right direction must be gaining power and control over the tongue (vv. 2b–5a). We need to take it over before it takes us over, always with disastrous consequences. There is a challenge in the use of *teleios* here (v. 2b), when it says those who do so become "perfect," as the word also means "mature." While we will never attain sinless perfection, we can reach spiritual maturity, and to do so we must avoid "stumbling" in our use of speech among God's people. The first two illustrations—the bit in a horse's mouth and the rudder on a ship—prepare for the third: the small spark causing the massive forest fire, which brings out the destructive potential of the tongue. The image of fiery destruction will dominate this entire section, and it is especially intended to prepare for the demonic use of the tongue to destroy God's work in the world. We all must be aware of how such savage results have been achieved throughout history. Satan is truly alive and well in the power of the tongue to destroy.

The three images in verses 2b–5a developed on the whole the positive power of the tongue to control things (the third moved into the negative realm to prepare for the rest), while the three in verses 6–12 show its terrible destructive power. James begins with a descending series of disastrous images (v. 6) that picture evil speech as a terrible conflagration consuming us entirely, moving from its evil power to corrupt to a devilish and hellish firestorm that destroys everything we have ever been and ever will be. This may be the most terrifying set of images in the whole letter, and if he was trying to scare us into making changes in our lives, he certainly succeeded.

In light of this danger, especially the idea of a spark burning down a forest, James develops the evil potential of the tongue to produce a destructive conflagration that consumes a community (v. 6). The images develop in a descending series that moves from bad to worse. It is first a devastating fire and then a "world of evil" that consumes the individual and through them the body of the church as a whole. Next, it "corrupts" us entirely and actually destroys the entire course of our existence, causing changes we are for the rest of our lives unable to overcome. The ups and downs of life become a cycle of pain and frustration. Finally, the tongue is "set on fire by hell," as Satan uses it to destroy us and the whole community of God's people. The tongue is a battleground that is at the heart of spiritual warfare.

The tongue is then pictured (vv. 7–8) as a wild, untamable animal, and while nearly the entire animal realm has been conquered by humankind, the tongue has not and will never be. However, this is so only from a human perspective. When we surrender entirely to God and learn to rely on him, he can and will gain power over the tongue and enable us to use it for good. However, in and of itself it will never rest but remain out of control, a destructive force that can kill.

Moreover, the tongue is duplicitous, one minute serving God in worship and the next pouring out filth at others (vv. 9–10). We cannot praise our "Lord and Father" out of one side of our mouth and yet curse people out of the other side. Such hypocrisy will bring serious judgment down on our heads. We dare not allow such a "double-minded" lifestyle (1:8) to consume us.

Finally, James uses three examples from nature to show the incompatibility of double-talk in the church. In the same way that fresh and salt water will never gush forth from the same spring, the same mouth should never be able to both bless and curse. Similarly, crops will always produce the fruit found in the seedlings. Olives and figs will spring forth from the type of seeds that are planted. In the same way, evil will proceed from an evil heart and the same with good coming out of a good heart. Finally, bitter water can only come from a bitter spring, so we must make sure we are godly and sweet in temperament, lest our tongues reflect our instability and wickedness. We will only turn around and use our speech for good after we have repented and got right with God. Both today as well as back then, the church needs revival. When we give ourselves entirely to God, we will find the strength to control our tongues.

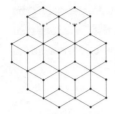

WISDOM FROM GOD IN THE MIDST OF CONFLICT

(3:13–4:12)

Returning to the point of 1:5–8, about the need for wisdom, James shows that the tongue will fail to achieve its God-given purpose until it is infused with God-given wisdom. Some think that this section is a group of isolated, independent sayings added artificially here by a later editor. However, it is quite closely related to both what precedes and what follows, and as I said at the start of the last chapter, 3:1–4:12 is a tightly constructed essay with an ABA pattern in which this central section provides the solution for an unchecked and problematic use of the tongue that leads to bickering and conflict in the church. Still, 3:13–18 is closely connected not just to this central section but to the letter as a whole. It is essential and central to the message of divinely given wisdom as the antidote for sin.

James returns to the qualifications of a teacher (from 3:1), adding the concept of wisdom from 1:5–8 as the key to successful teaching and ministry. Moreover, he does not just have the leaders in mind here. While they are more guilty of misusing the tongue, the church as a whole is guilty of dissension and conflict. So while the teachers are strongly behind both 3:1–12 and 13–18, the lay members of the church are addressed as well. All people in the church, but especially the leaders, need to seek the "wisdom that comes from heaven" rather than that earthly, inadequate wisdom that too easily leads to fractured churches.

TRUE WISDOM COMES FROM GOD (3:13–18)

WISDOM SHOWN BY DEEDS (3:13)

This begins by challenging the readers, especially the teachers among them, to consider seriously their attitudes and motivations, specifically to ask if they are "wise and understanding" of God's ways. Knowledge is clearly not enough; it must be coupled with the wisdom sent from God. *Epistēmōn* refers to a person who combines technical knowledge or theory with practice, who puts it to work practically in achieving results. This builds on being "wise" (*sophos*), connoting the use of this knowledge to attain certain goals or purposes. In Deuteronomy 1:13, 15, knowledge and wisdom are leadership qualities for helping God's people obey his laws. The divinely given wisdom enables the leader to apply understanding to the correct conduct it is supposed to produce. So James is calling for these church leaders to identify what is right in the eyes of God and guide the church into the conduct that puts it into practice.

In the second half of the verse he seeks a practical demonstration or proof of this God-led wisdom—namely, good deeds combined with humility. A truly wise Christ follower will prove themselves "by their good life, by deeds done in the humility that comes from wisdom." Living the "good life" today has perverted the meaning here. Today "the good life" centers on pleasure and narcissistic luxury, but in James it refers to an honorable life lived for God and good works. To "show" it (*deixatō*) would be to "demonstrate" or "prove" to everyone who sees you that you have godly wisdom, and your life is guided by it. In 1 Peter this is a major theme, meant to disprove the slander of the ungodly and bring them to Christ (1 Pet 2:12, 15, 19; 3:1–2, 10–11, 16). Literally, "good life" is "good conduct," meaning that the good works are not occasional acts but become a lifestyle of goodness that defines everything you do.

These deeds are done "in the humility of wisdom," with *sophias* (as the NIV shows) a genitive of source, "the humility that comes from wisdom." This mandate for humility or meekness (*prautēs*) rarely appears in the **Hellenistic** world, for to the Greeks, meekness was weakness. But Jesus was the embodiment of the meek servant, saying, "I am gentle and humble in heart" (Matt 11:29), and he made meekness one of the most important Christian virtues: "Blessed are the meek" (Matt 5:5). Meekness is a gentle spirit that turns the saints into servants and enables them to care for others. It is shown to God (1:21, "humbly accept the word planted in you") and to people around us (here). For James, this "wisdom" is the good *yetzer*, or impulse (see comments on 1:14), which struggles against the evil impulses of 3:14–16 and 4:1–3. True good works are impossible without the wisdom to identify good from bad and to put them into practice in the correct manner at the proper time.

WORLDLY WISDOM (3:14–16)

In total contrast to this meek divine wisdom is the aggressive "bitter envy and selfish ambition" of the world exemplified in all too many Christians (3:14). "If" here is another condition of fact (= "since," see 2:8, 9; 3:3), leading into the theme of dissension that will dominate 3:14–4:12. Many translate "bitter envy" (*zēlon pikron*) as "harsh zeal," and it is possible that a zealous jealousy is the thrust here. Such people are aggressively narcissistic, and that self-centeredness makes them envious of anyone who has anything good in their lives. When God is "jealous" (Exod 20:5; Deut 4:24; Josh 24:19), he is concerned for the holiness of his name, but when people are jealous they care only for their possessions and status in society. "Envy" is wanting what belongs to someone else with no regard for their good or their rights. It leads to that feeling that we deserve the windfall or luxurious item a lot more than the

other person, and it often results in doing harm to them in order
to procure what is rightfully theirs.

James adds "bitter" along with "selfish ambition" to draw out
the contentious side of their actions. The result of their behavior
is a fractured church split apart by selfish leaders whose rampant
love for self leads them to fight bitterly whenever they don't get
their way. The resultant tension produces the poisonous tongue
of 3:8, which destroys the unity of the community. The "selfish
ambition" (eritheia) is a "party spirit," not a desire for wild "parties" but an atmosphere that contains within itself the nuance of
a willingness to split the group into warring "parties" in order to
win the argument. The term is used of the sins of the Corinthians
(2 Cor 12:20), the dissension in Philippi (Phil 2:3), and those who
will face God's wrath (Rom 2:8; Gal 5:20). This desire for power
and prestige sows discord into the entire community, and such
will face God's strong disfavor. As we will see in 4:1–3, such attitudes turn the tongue into a weapon of war.

Those who allow such sinful kinds of behavior to gain control
of them are challenged not to "boast about it or deny the truth" that
they are under indictment from God. Boasting is a dominant characteristic of such selfish ambition, but while the world may laud
such conduct, it is the height of foolishness in light of God's displeasure. There is no place for pride in this attitude and behavior, for
it is based on a false claim to "wisdom" (3:13). As in Jeremiah 9:23–
24, "Let not the wise boast of their wisdom ... or the rich boast of
their riches, but let the one who boasts boast about this: that they
have the understanding to know me, that I am the LORD." There is
a place for pride and boasting among the saints, but it will never
be a boasting centered on self, but only on God and others.

Those who boast selfishly do nothing other than "deny the
truth," literally "lie against the truth." They cover up the reality
and pretend to be giving God's truth, but in reality the only wisdom
they demonstrate is a worldly wisdom, devoid of understanding
from God and filled with selfish desires and goals. This is even

more true in our fame-obsessed culture, for all too many have made themselves millionaires on the basis not of serving the Lord but by exemplifying a charisma that is entirely of the world. There is no "truth" behind it, and the only "glory" they seek is their own.

God's wisdom "comes from heaven" (3:17), part of the "good gifts" that are sent from heaven in 1:17-18. However, the pretentious wisdom of these worldly people has nothing in common with true wisdom. Instead, it is "earthly, unspiritual, demonic."

These three adjectives form a downward spiral. Rather than originating from heaven, this false wisdom is entirely "earthly" (*epigeios*), not only an entity that has its origin in this world but one that is the total antithesis of what belongs to God's realm. This wisdom rejects the things of God and desires only what belongs to this world. Next, it is "unspiritual," or "sensual," not in a sexual way but belonging to that which pertains only to this "natural" (*psychikos*) realm. It is the mark of the natural person, produced by the unregenerate mind and has nothing of God in it. Finally, it is "demonic," or "devilish," its true source not even of this world but from Satan and his minions. As in 3:6, it is "set on fire by hell," demonically inspired and controlled. The two sources of temptation are combined here—self and Satan. These three sources of false wisdom parallel the three classic sources of evil: "the world, the flesh, and the devil."

James concludes the negative side of this false wisdom in verse 16 by reiterating the results of such "envy and selfish ambition" (from v. 14). Flowing out of their serious spiritual problem— namely, their self-centered, power-hungry aspirations, which have brought backbiting and chaos to the church—God's people have had to endure "disorder and every evil practice." "Disorder" (*akatastasia*) recalls the instability of 1:8 and the uncontrollable tongue of 3:8 and pictures a complete breakdown of order, as in the "wars and uprisings" of Luke 21:9, which describes the last days. In the terrible selfishness of all too many leaders, the church receives a sad foretaste of the tumultuous chaos of the last days. We are living in a time in which truth itself is rejected, and everyone seems to believe they have the right to decide for themselves what truth is. Anarchy is no longer just a political stance but has become a way of life, and truth itself has died an ignominious death at the hands of an entire generation of self-oriented thinkers.

Moreover, this false wisdom will also entail the "evil practice," or "vile deeds," of the realm of darkness entering the church. The sins of the tongue have brought the world into the church, and terrible dissension has taken over. Some think this refers to lawsuits, Christians taking one another to court and shaming each other publicly, as in 1 Corinthians 6:1–8. However, that is only a single aspect, for James refers to "*every* evil practice" and so must include all types of incendiary speech and slander.

HEAVENLY WISDOM (3:17–18)

James has just told what heavenly wisdom is not, and now he turns and tells what it is. This is a beautifully written, near-poetic paean to wisdom, presenting the attributes of the God-centered person. One could almost call this a hymn to wisdom very much like the hymn to love in 1 Corinthians 13:4–7.

The false wisdom is "earthly [and] unspiritual," while this true wisdom is "first of all pure." The four following characteristics develop aspects of this purity: they all begin with *e*, and the last two end with -*kritos*. The emphasis is not on the purity laws of the Torah but on moral blamelessness with a clear conscience. Such a person is the opposite of the worldly characterized by verses 15–16. This person entails an absence of sin and defilement, true holiness. There is a spiritual and moral faithfulness to God leading to a divinely directed way of life that glorifies God and serves his people in his messianic community.

The other six qualities are introduced by *epeita* (then) and provide aspects of this moral and spiritual purity. In the context of serious dissension in the community, "peace-loving," or "peaceable," is another key attribute of godly wisdom. This quality will become the theme of 3:18. There is a complete absence of peace in 14–16, while it is central here and builds on Matthew 5:9, "Blessed are the peacemakers" (see also Ps 34:14; Isa 52:7; Rom 12:18; Heb 12:11). This is the exact opposite of the jealous, combative ambition that produces the "fights and quarrels" of 4:1. Peace with God is achieved through the cross and the gift of salvation; peace with the people around us is the product of sanctification—that is, the process of holiness. As the Spirit enters us and draws us to God both in our thinking and our actions, love takes over, and as God's love infiltrates our being, our relations with those around us change correspondingly.

"Considerate," or "gentle" (*epieikēs*), in the Greek mind means "reasonable" or "fair" but for Christians refers to that spirit that refuses to demand its own rights but lives for others (also Phil 4:5; 1 Tim 3:3). So it connotes an empathetic, forbearing spirit that accepts others as they are and is willing to forgive. Next, this God-sent wisdom is "submissive" (*eupeithēs*), or "open to reason" (RSV, ESV), or "accommodating" (NET). This "willingness to yield to others" (NLT) is the direct opposite of the narcissistic concerns of verses 14–16 and is the epitome of the self-giving spirit that is supposed to characterize the Christ follower. The term only appears here in the New Testament, but the quality is illustrated in Romans 14:1–15:13, where Paul tells both the strong and the weak that they must respect one another and defer to the religious sensitivities of each other. This is so needed today, as Christians fight and disrespect each other over every issue imaginable.

The final three continue this emphasis on godly wisdom lived out in our lives. "Full of mercy and good fruit" reverses the sinful results of the counterfeit wisdom above. Instead of a tongue "full of deadly poison" (3:8), we have a life "full of mercy"—namely, caring and sharing with the needy around us. Such acts of love and compassion reflect a kind spirit concretely via good deeds, which indicates the presence of the Spirit in our lives. Mercy is known by its "good fruit" and is the natural by-product of the "word implanted in you" (1:21).

Finally, the saint filled with heavenly wisdom is "impartial and sincere." The first (*adiakritos*) stands opposed both to the double-mindedness of 1:6, 8, and the partiality of 2:4. This person refuses to discriminate and both treats and respects everyone equally. It is immensely difficult to exemplify this godly trait consistently, for we are all sinful, selfish creatures, and only those truly filled with the Spirit and holiness can do so. The final trait, "sincere," or "without pretense and hypocrisy" (*anypokritos*), is closely connected. Such a person refuses to play-act and consistently exhibits godly qualities. There is no hiding behind a mask for such people, and they live out what they claim to stand for.

The concluding description of godly wisdom (3:18) returns to the beginning of the verse and is an **inclusio** with the "peace-loving" person described there. Those with true wisdom will always "sow [seeds of] peace" and then through that "reap a harvest of righteousness." This is not another characteristic of wisdom but the by-product of wisdom. So verse 17 defines wisdom, and then verse 18 tells what its effects will be. Here we have the antidote for the epidemic of divisiveness and dissension caused by rampant self-centeredness, the main problem of 3:1–4:12. If our speech ever begins to sow seeds of peace in our assemblies, the "fights and quarrels" of the next verse (4:1) would never take place. Divine wisdom calls for peace-loving gardeners (3:17) who sow peace rather than discord (3:18) in God's vineyard (see also Rom 14:19; Heb 12:14), producing a life that truly will make a difference.

What is sown in peace produces a "harvest of righteousness." *Dikaiosynē* (righteousness) is used ethically here to refer not to right standing before God but to the righteous behavior that flows out of it. The genitive "of" in this instance is epexegetical, meaning it gives additional explanation. Thus the phrase can be translated "a harvest—namely, right conduct in the presence of God."[1]

---

1. This is better in this context than seeing it as descriptive ("righteous harvest") or objective ("a harvest producing righteousness").

We will have a bumper crop of spiritual victory and live in a way that greatly pleases God, beginning with peace rather than conflict in our community.

JAMES CONNECTS SPEECH AND CHURCH CONFLICT (4:1-12)

James now gives us a practical example of what arises when false wisdom operates—war in the church. Dissension takes over, and catastrophe results. Some have taken 4:1-10 as a new unit centered on worldliness in the church and the factious people who cause it. However, the themes are so closely tied to both 3:1-12 and 13-18 that it is clear to take this with those earlier sections as a triad of paragraphs on conflict in the church. I find another ABA pattern in this subsection: A: friendship with the world (vv. 1-6); B: the solution—submission to God (vv. 7-10); A': worldly conflict (vv. 11-12).

THE SOURCE OF CONFLICT (4:1-6)

Origins of internal strife (4:1-2a)

James is so upset with his readers for giving in to their baser emotions and dividing the church that he begins by indicting them with a rhetorical question: "What causes fights and quarrels among you?" There is a serious discord resulting in strife, the polar opposite of peace-loving wisdom in 3:17-18. Moreover, the tongue is at the center of it all. I still prefer the traditional "wars and fightings" (KJV) to "fights and quarrels" (NIV), for these people are engaging in no-holds-barred attacks against each other. The language in these verses is so strong that some say it could not have been written to a young church early in the first century. I disagree, but agree that the language and imagery are incredibly severe. In fact, some think there is actual violence behind these images, as people in the early 60s engaged in Zealot activity. That would be possible if this were a later letter, but I don't think it is, and therefore James is more likely referring to verbal sparring (perhaps fistfights) rather than more physically harmful violence.

He immediately answers his own query: "Don't they come from your desires that battle within you?" The term for "desires" is a strong one, *hedonōn*, "passions, lusts," from which the English word "hedonism" is derived. James is implying that they simply enjoy fighting and so want to slander each other. This recalls the same thrust in 1:13–15, the source of temptation being the "evil desires" in people. The "lusts" here are not sexual in nature but are still the product of living entirely for self and personal pleasure rather than God. It is these that "battle within you" or, more literally, "make war in your members," with likely a double meaning— fighting within individuals takes over their actions and causes corporate wars among the members in the church. This pictures hedonistic pleasure as an invading army trying to destroy us both individually and corporately.

These next verses (4:2–3) describe the progression of sin as it destroys God's people piece by piece. There is a well-known difference of opinion as to how to translate verse 2. Some (KJV, NIV 1984, LEB, NET, some commentators) have placed a period after the negative clauses, creating a three-part structure:

> You want something but don't get it.
> You kill and covet, but you cannot have what you want.
> You quarrel and fight.

Others (NASB, NRSV, REB, NIV 2011, ESV, NLT, the majority of commentators) place the period after the results and have a two-part structure:

> You desire but do not have, so you kill.
> You covet but you cannot get what you want, so you quarrel and fight.

The second translation possibility is the superior option, for in the first one, the progression "kill and covet" does not make a great deal of sense. Moreover, the second contains a slightly better parallelism. The idea of an escalating conflict is featured in the first option, while in the second, selfish ambition and envy are highlighted, building on the sinful, false "wisdom" of 3:14–16. The progression of James's thinking in this central section (3:1–4:12) is served very well in this second structure. Here we see that the conflict that has decimated the community is the natural result of their worldly perspective, their desire to obtain what is not theirs. "Kill" here is not literal but metaphorical, the result of slander that destroys people's reputation. Matthew 5:22 describes anger as murder in the mind. James is making a similar point here. These shallow Christians would like to get rid of those who have more than they and to take over what naturally belongs to these others.

James here traces the wicked path that their self-centered desires have taken. They demand what they don't have and are filled with envy over what is not supposed to be theirs, both in terms of possessions and power over the community. They proceed from anger to jealousy in the two sentences. Several scholars have seen a **chiasm** in the developing ideas of 4:1–2:

> A fights and quarrels
> > B from evil desires
> > B′ from frustrated envy
> A′ quarrel and fight (note the reverse order here)

Their frustration should lead to repentance, but instead it results in even more conflict because of the intense envy they feel. This is the portrait of the natural person—when they don't get what their sinful desires demand, they try to take it by any means possible. They have become the antithesis of the kind of leader and teacher God desires.

Reasons for unanswered prayer (4:2b–3)

In light of these false motives and desires, these people have not received any answers to prayer. In verses 2b–3 James provides two reasons why God is silent: "You do not have because you do not ask God. When you ask, you do not receive, because you ask with wrong motives, that you may spend what you get on your pleasures." Christ had promised that his followers would receive what they asked for (Matt 7:7–8), but now James tells them that they are so consumed with getting what they want that they fail even to ask God for it.

In other words, there is no trust or dependence on God, only an obsession with their selfish demands. They have forgotten 1:5: "if any of you lacks wisdom [or anything else], you should ask God, who gives generously." God is left out of the formula, and all they care about is what they desire. This is a very important reminder for us in our consumer society. We have so much, more actually than anyone else in all of history. This should have produced a contented people, but it has only produced more greed. Sinful people simply cannot have enough of the world's resources and as a result have forgotten about God, and that includes all of us all too often!

The second reminder is that even when we do pray, we "ask with wrong motives." Again, our consumer mentality leads us to ignore our provider and center only on the product. Our motives are all screwed up by the "affluenza" that has afflicted us. Moreover, none of the things desired are heavenly in origin. They want only earthly commodities, so God is left out of the process at both ends. They aren't trusting him, only demanding things from him, and their demands are not for spiritual or eternal commodities but earthly, temporary, material products. They do not want to serve God or care for his people, only to "spend what you get on your pleasures." God will not respond to such selfishness or give them what will only destroy them spiritually. Prayer itself has been degraded into idolatry and hedonistic pleasure seeking.

This certainly reminds us of the "health and wealth" gospel, that dangerous movement that has turned materialism and greed into a religion.

Result: friendship with the world (4:4-6)

These verses begin with a strong denunciation of the readers: "You adulterous people." Literally, he calls them "adulteresses" (*moichalides*), alluding to the Old Testament view of Israel as "the bride of Yahweh" (Isa 54:5-6; 61:10; 62:1-5; compare the "bride of Christ" in Eph 5:25-27; Rev 19:7-8; 21:2, 9), who then committed adultery against their Lord/husband (Isa 57:3, 7-8; Jer 3:6, 20; 13:27; Ezek 16:35-38; Hos 9:1). The prophet Hosea embodied this spiritual infidelity in a tragic way, being told to marry the prostitute Gomer as a symbol of Israel prostituting herself with foreign gods. So James is accusing many readers of being "adulteresses" in seeking pleasure and the world over God.

These arrogant, greedy pleasure-seekers were thinking they could accommodate "friendship with the world" with their claim to be Christians. At every turn they acted consistently against the way of Christ—their failure to live out what they seemingly believed (1:22-25) or to care for the needy (1:27), their prejudice in favor of the rich over the poor (2:1-13), a refusal to work out their faith with good deeds (2:14-26), a desire for the higher-status positions in the church (3:1), abuse of their God-given gift of speech to slander others (3:2-12), selfish ambition and envy (3:14, 16), serious conflict in the church (4:1-2), capitulation to hedonistic pleasures (4:1, 3), backbiting (4:11-12). The litany of sins seems unceasing; no wonder James is beside himself with righteous indignation. These people have not denounced Christ, but their conduct seems to disavow him in favor of the world's ways, and we will see in 5:19-20 that many of them are moving in the direction of apostasy!

In Hellenism the idea of "friendship" connoted a very serious relationship with political and social allegiance and a harmony of outlook, sharing the same standards and seeking the same plea-sures. James's readers have chosen the world rather than Christ for that unity of perspective and so stand in "enmity against God." By its very nature, to be a "friend of the world" means to be "an enemy of God." He states this twice for emphasis (see 1 John 2:15). When we give our heart to the world, we commit spiritual adultery and become God's enemies, living under his wrath and directing ourselves toward divine judgment. To prefer the world is to turn against God and be subject to his covenant curses.

God as our husband reacts jealously when we are unfaith-ful to him and follow the world's practices. He wants more for us and both grieves and is filled with wrath when we cheat on him with our lifestyle and conduct. Translating the quotation in verse 5 is immensely difficult, for the Greek can be translated three ways, each of them viable and preferred by some transla-tions and scholars:

1. The spirit God has caused to live in us is filled with envy (NLT, NIV 1984, REB, LEB, NET).
2. God jealously longs for the spirit he has caused to dwell in us (NIV 2011, NASB, NRSV, ESV).
3. The Spirit God has caused to live in us opposes our envy (NLT margin).

Since all three make sense, we must decide based on context. Which one fits best in this section of James? The third is unlikely, for this letter has not mentioned the Spirit yet, and there is no hint of anything like this in the immediate context. The first is very viable and fits well the envy of 3:14, 16; 4:2. The term *phtho-nos* normally connotes human jealousy or envy (Rom 1:29; Gal 5:21; Phil 1:15; 1 Pet 2:1). However, the second also makes a great deal of sense, as we will see, and I believe the second option is the best one.

The emphasis is on our relationship with God in 4:4, 6–8, and so God would be a natural subject. Moreover, there is a great deal in Scripture about the jealousy of God for his people. Exodus 20:5 states, "You shall not bow down to [idols] or worship them; for I, the LORD your God, am a jealous God" (also Exod 34:14; Deut 4:24; Josh 24:19–20; Isa 26:11; Ezek 16:42; Nah 1:2; Zech 8:2). "The spirit he has caused to dwell in us" refers to the creation of humankind in the image of God and their bearing the "spirit" or breath of life given at creation. Since God loves us as his bride, he is jealous of us when we stray after other gods and the world. This results in two things: his anger and his desire to bring us to repentance and forgive us. This is the meaning of "he gives us more grace" in verse 6.

But it is unclear which passage of Scripture James is referring to in his citation, for there are none with that wording. He might have been referring to Exodus 20:5 or any of the others listed in the previous paragraph. Some believe that the quotation includes verse 6a ("he gives us more grace") and points forward to the Proverbs 3:34 quotation in the second half of the verse. But that would be clumsy, as the verse would be quoted differently in two successive sentences. I agree with those who believe it is not a single passage but a collage, and that James is citing a scriptural "theme" here.

Since God is a loving and compassionate husband, seeks our repentance, and wants to forgive, he "gives us more grace." These grace gifts are the "good and perfect gift[s]" of 1:17, the strength and inner resources from the Spirit's empowering presence that enable us to overcome the world's negative influences. If we just had 4:4–5, we would despair, for the forces against us are too strong, and the sins of all of us deserve only God's wrath. However, his grace and mercy in sending his Son and the Holy Spirit make it possible to be overcomers (Rom 8:37; Rev 2:7, 11, 17, 26; 3:5, 12, 21). While we falter, God is ever there and never tires. He provides what we lack, the strength to persevere (Jas 1:4, 12).

God's gracious response is more than sufficient, but he demands our response in turn—namely, a humble dependence on him. For this James cites Proverbs 3:34: "God opposes the proud but shows favor to the humble" (also in 1 Pet 5:5). The grace of God is given to the humble rather than the arrogant. The humble are those who relinquish control of their lives, learn to rely entirely on the Triune Godhead, and seek at all times to be faithful to him rather than surrender to the world. The "proud" are those who rely on self, live for pleasure, and prefer the world over God. Thus God is "opposed" to them, and they will experience only his wrath (see Pss 18:27; 34:18; Prov 6:17; 16:5, 18; Isa 61:1; Zeph 3:11–12).

SOLUTION: SUBMISSION TO GOD (4:7–10)

The poles: God or Satan (4:7–8a)

James employs another ABA pattern here (see introductions to 3:13–18; 4:1–12): A: submit to God; B: resist the devil; A': come near to God. Here A also = the means and B = the results. This is how God's people overcome friendship with the world. Since God pours out his grace on the humble (v. 6), it is essential that they submit entirely to him. So this is how Proverbs 3:34 is enacted in the church. As his people place themselves under God's controlling presence (the meaning of the imperative *hypotagēte*), they experience his grace gifts and find victory. This is how we hear and obey (1:22–25) and add works to our faith (2:14–26).

We become "friends" rather than "enemies" of God (4:4) when we utterly submit and experience his favor (4:6). Two aspects of the Lord's Prayer parallel this (Matt 6:9–10): "hallowed be your name" or "may your name be kept holy," an absolute concern that the sacredness and glory of the name of the Lord be central in your life; and "your will be done," a complete surrender to God's will in everything you say and do. Every area of your life must be dedicated to the glory of his name.

When this happens, we have the strength to "resist the devil." *Diabolō* means "enemy" or "adversary," the being who is in absolute antithesis to everything that God stands for and the one who seeks to destroy us and turn us away from God. His story is told in Revelation 12:1–10. He was that (arch?)angel, called "the dragon," who stood against God and seduced one-third of the angelic realm to rebel, then with his fallen angels was cast out of heaven to earth by Michael and the good angels, who remained faithful to God. Throughout history he has been "filled with [frustrated] fury" (Rev 12:11) and tries to destroy God's work in us and the world.

We have no chance against him in our own strength, and our only hope is to place ourselves under the Lord and receive that strength sufficient to find victory. We are able to "resist" or "stand against" him only when empowered by the Spirit. Moreover, when we have truly submitted to God, we must resist Satan and all he stands for. We cannot submit to God and yield to Satan at the same time. The Lord's Prayer includes "lead us not into temptation," which actually means, "do not let us yield to temptation" (Matt 6:13). Faithfulness to God means a refusal to surrender to temptation, trusting the Lord to give us the spiritual strength to overcome (1 Cor 10:13). When we do this, we are promised that "he will flee" from us. The devil knows when he is overmatched, and as he did when Christ opposed him, he could only leave "until an opportune time" (Luke 4:13). Satan is not an overpowering figure who cannot be defeated. Christ has won the victory, and when we submit to him and receive his power in us, we too will be victorious.

Submission in 4:7a is now paralleled in 4:8 with "come near to God." The command "draw near" (*engisate*) is the primary verb for worship, as at Sinai (Exod 19:21 LXX), the altar or sanctuary (Lev 21:21, 23; Num 8:19 LXX), or "approaching" the Lord himself (Ezek 40:46 LXX). James's words here point forward to verse 9, drawing near in repentance as an essential part of submission. You can neither surrender to God nor resist the devil until you have mourned for your moral and spiritual failures. When you do so, you are assured that he will "come near to you" and forgive your sins, then pour his strength into you.

The meaning of repentance (4:8b–9)

So we turn now specifically to the basis for drawing near to God: repentance. As several interpreters have pointed out, James combines the external side ("purify your hands") with the internal side ("purify your hearts") of repentance. This is Old Testament language from the purity laws and means we need to get our actions and our thought lives right with God before we can truly begin a life of submission and obedience. These members of the church, as we have seen, are in serious trouble with God, and James calls them "sinners" and "double-minded." He can no longer call them "brothers and sisters," for their problems are too serious.

The "double-minded" goes back to the charge in 1:8 that they have become people of the world more than followers of God. The problem is their divided loyalty, as they are giving to God only a small portion of their true selves. Their divided mind is especially evident in 4:4, where James castigates their "friendship to the world." Their problem is at the heart of depraved humanity, with their minds far from God.

Things are so serious that James demands they be totally filled with sorrow for the sins they have committed. The staccato impression given by the three commands "Grieve, mourn and wail" is a powerful call to public sorrow for sin. Let us unpack the call. The first refers to a deep distress and misery induced by a terrible tragedy, here the sin that has taken you away from God. The second calls for a period of public mourning for that separation from God. And the third is the actual loud weeping caused by the mourning. The three are near synonyms and demand a level of public repentance that is made evident to all around. These shallow Christians are being given a choice: grieve now and get right with God, or face eternal grief at the last judgment. It is not enough to sorrow privately; private repentance must become corporate. James is calling for revival.

In their sinful sojourn in the world (4:4), they have often participated in the false laughter and joy of their prideful boasting and pleasure seeking (3:14–26). Such worldly frivolity must stop, for it will lead to eternal judgment (Luke 6:25). This is the laughter and joy of fools (Eccl 7:6) and must be replaced with mourning and gloom. They weren't just treating their sinful practices lightly. They were ignoring them altogether in their pursuit of hedonistic fun, power plays, and worldly success. James joins Jesus in demanding this reversal: "Blessed are you who weep now, for you will laugh. ... Woe to you who laugh now, for you will mourn and weep" (Luke 6:21, 25).

True joy can only come after one has sought and found forgiveness, and too often modern preachers ignore this in their false desire to make people feel good about themselves when they have no right to do so. Such preachers are virtually allowing parishioners to go to hell thinking God will accept them in spite of their serious sins. The threefold path is clear here, and it will result in true, eternal joy and laughter—cast off your worldly so-called joy, sorrow deeply for sin, and get right with God. Turn to the joy of the Spirit and truly rejoice. Then we are "friends with God" for eternity.

The means: humble submission (4:10)

James returns to verse 7, calling for a complete abandonment of worldly pride and a casting of ourselves totally at the feet of the Godhead in repentance and submission. The poles were set in 3:13–14—selfish ambition versus humility. Exalt self or glorify God; you cannot have both in your life (as with praising God and cursing people in 3:9–10). If the two sides in conflict (4:1–2) discover humility, the infighting will cease as love takes over. Once you "humble yourselves before the Lord," James tells his readers, power struggles will dissipate and turn into love fests as a spirit of fellowship envelops both sides. As Jesus says in Mark 9:35, "Anyone who wants to be first must be the very last, and the servant of all" (see also Mark 10:43; Matt 23:12). Without humility, community is not possible.

When we stop seeking our own power and glory and get right with God and those around us, then we will truly find our greatness. When we lift ourselves up, we fail and become fools. Temporary, earth-centered glory can never suffice. When we have thrown ourselves on the Lord in repentance and humility, then "he will lift you up," both now and in eternity. The options are clear—self-glory or glorify God and wait for him to glorify us. Do we prefer temporary attention from other sinners like us or eternal praise from our God?

THE SIN OF BACKBITING AND JUDGING (4:11–12)

James now returns to the sins of the tongue, applying this material to the problems that are in danger of destroying the community. He once more addresses them as "brothers and sisters" to show he regards them as family members under God (in contrast to 4:4, 8). The power struggles have come full circle, combining the discrimination of 2:1–13 with the slander of 3:1–12, as these Christians "slander one another" (*katalaleō*, the same verb translated "speak against" in the next clause). This type of speech includes many kinds of verbal attacks—slander, backbiting, gossip, mocking, spreading rumors, maligning, and so on. The desire is to destroy another person's reputation and turn others against them. This misuse of the tongue has always been considered one of the worst forms of sin (Exod 23:1; Lev 19:16; Ps 15:3; Prov 10:18; 11:13; Matt 29:19).

There is a huge difference between judging and admonishing others. Judging, on the one hand, involves looking down on people and enjoying telling them their faults. There is an absence of love or compassion. Admonishing, on the other hand, involves standing alongside others in love and trying to restore them to the Lord (Gal 6:1). It is redemptive at the core and helps them defeat sin in their lives (Heb 3:13). There are no feelings of superiority, and no gossip or slander. The problem with James's readers is the conflict and power struggles behind it all.

The point here is that to slander and judge others entails turning against the law[2] and judging it. What does this mean? The law

---

2. As we have seen before (1:25; 2:8–12), the "law" here is considered from a new-covenant perspective, the Mosaic law fulfilled in Christ and transformed into the Torah of the Messiah.

is clear regarding the sin of slander (see above), and to ignore the Torah injunction and "sin with a high hand" against it is to place yourself in judgment over it and regard it as insignificant. In fact, to do so is to sin against the "royal law" of God (2:8). To willingly slander others is to sin against God's laws. They are not "keeping" the law but "sitting in judgment on it," especially its central command to "love your neighbor" in Leviticus 19:18 (just after the injunction not to slander in v. 16). This person places themselves above the law and thereby "speaks against" it by ignoring it.

The issue is not just the law (v. 11), but the very character of God (v. 12) is at stake, for he alone is the "one Lawgiver and Judge." So they are not just ignoring the law; they are replacing God at the head of it. God is the only rightful Judge, and they have usurped his place by interpreting the law at their whim. By encroaching on territory reserved for God, they are deliberately forgetting that all truth stems from him, and their only proper task is to accept and obey. They will never be "lawgivers"; only God can perform that function (see Ps 94:2; 1 Cor 4:5; 2 Tim 4:8; Heb 12:23).

As the supreme Judge, only God is "able to save and destroy," which they ignore to their peril. God in Christ alone is Savior (1 Sam 4:3; Pss 7:10; 18:2; Luke 19:10; Heb 7:25), and he alone can eternally destroy (Pss 5:6; 17:14; Isa 11:14; Jer 25:9; 1 Cor 3:17). Those who repent and submit entirely to God will be saved, while those who continue in their arrogant rebellion will be destroyed. The conclusion has a note of contempt to it: "who are you to judge your neighbor?" (see Rom 2:1; 14:4). The sarcasm is obvious. By setting themselves up as judges, they were judged by the true Judge.

––––––

With 3:13–18 we reached the heart of the letter of James, for it is the primary example of New Testament Wisdom literature. In 1:5–8 wisdom was the means by which we could turn trials into times of spiritual growth and maturity, and here it is the means by

which we can turn the tongue from an instrument of evil and dissension into an instrument of good works. In verse 13 it is defined
as that God-given "understanding" that enables us to "show" or
demonstrate all the practical good that can flow from the tongue
in the church.

In this section James demonstrates the radical opposition
between worldly (3:14–16) and heavenly (vv. 17–18) wisdom. The
worldly type is characterized by a narcissistic envy and ambition
that seeks only earthly reward and only for the benefit of yourself. Such an earth-centered perspective is doomed from the start,
for it will only proceed from bad to worse, being first "earthly"
or concerned only with the worldly side of life, then "unspiritual" or belonging only to the natural rather than the supernatu-
ral realm of reality, and finally "demonic," guided and controlled
by Satan himself.

The final result of worldly wisdom is chaos (v. 16), as such self-
oriented thinking will always produce dissension, and everyone
will demand their own way and fight anyone who disagrees. This
type of conflict was at the heart of James's churches and is no less
a problem today. When both the leadership and the lay members
of the church refuse to give an inch to each other and demand that
everyone acquiesce to their half-baked ideas, peace and joy disappear from the church, and everything falls apart. Such an earth-
centered perspective should never characterize believers, for every
aspect of it is antithetical to the ways of God.

In contrast to this, heavenly wisdom (vv. 17–18) provides seven
qualities that should be at the heart of every saint. These are the
ways of God, and when inculcated into our lives, they turn us into
world-changers. The two primary characteristics are purity, which
is the true lifestyle of the godly person, and peace-loving, which is
the result of pure Christian conduct on relationships in the community. The other qualities flow out of these two and tell how
they are lived out in the body of Christ, the messianic community.
Such people are always centered on others rather than themselves

and have a true servant's heart in their single-minded devotion to those around them.

The next section returns to the problem behind this letter, the misuse of the tongue (3:1-12) that causes conflict and dissension in the church (4:1-12). There is another ABA pattern inside this material, as friendship with the world (4:1-6) and the conflict it causes (vv. 11-12) can only be overcome with submission to God (vv. 7-10). In the opening part of this section (vv. 1-3), James traces the origin of the dissension: the selfish ambition and envy of the "old self" (see Rom 6:6; Eph 4:22; Col 3:9), which demands for itself what others have. This is why their prayers are not being granted, because first of all they are not praying but thinking only of the pleasures they demand for themselves, and second, when they do pray they focus only on these pleasures and not on God. God will not acquiesce to such prayers.

As a result they have become a "friend of the world" and thus "an enemy of God" (vv. 4-6). You cannot be both; to follow the world's ways is to turn against God. God, however, is a jealous husband who demands that we be faithful in our actions as well as our beliefs. However, as a loving husband he gives us even greater strength so we can overcome our worldly proclivities and live godly lives.

The solution is both simple and profound (vv. 7-10)—submit to God by drawing near in full repentance, and then he will provide the strength to resist the devil and conquer the self-centered tendencies he causes to grow in us. Repentance is critical and demands a deep sorrow for sin that leads us to prostrate ourselves before God in full surrender. As we cast ourselves at the feet of our Lord, he then lifts us up and enables us to rise above the petty things of this world in order to glorify his name. Then he will give us victory and bring us glory, a glory that will be eternal.

It is clear in James's conclusion (vv. 11-12) what the problem is. When they slander each other, they are not just sinning against one another but against God and his law. They are setting themselves in God's place as Judge and replacing him as the "judge" of the law. Only he can be the true Judge of the law, and he is the Judge of us as well. So when they turn against God's demands by sitting in judgment of each other, they are bringing the true Judge down on their heads in judgment against them.

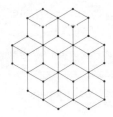

WARNINGS TO THE
WORLDLY AND THE WISE
(4:13–5:11)

The last major section in James begins here (4:13–5:11), and it
returns to the issue of poverty and wealth from 1:9–11; 2:1–13.
The vast majority of James's readers are poverty-stricken, but
much of the section addresses the wealthy (4:13–5:6), warning
them of the retribution they will face for misusing their wealth
and living for their riches rather than for God. There are three sections in this material, and the first two are introduced the same
way: "Now listen, you."

James addresses the wealthy in 4:13–5:6, and the poor in 5:7–11.
The primary interpretive debate in this section is whether 4:13–17
is addressing rich Christians or non-Christians. Wealthy unbelievers are definitely the subject in 5:1–6, and the similar opening
phrase in 4:13 and 5:1, "Now listen, you," has led some to conclude
that both passages have the same audience—namely, the pagan
wealthy class—with 4:13–17 challenging merchants and 5:1–6 landowners. If that is the case, this section is a diatribe denouncing
the ungodly rich who ignore God (4:13–17) and mistreat his pov-
erty-laden people (5:1–6). However, the actual tone of 4:13–17 goes
against this conclusion. James challenges the wealthy merchants
in this first segment to consider God's will (v. 15) and tells them

that down deep they know "the good they ought to do" (v. 17). He would say neither to the ungodly, and the tone of the two sections is radically different, with 5:1–6 a dire denunciation of the evil landowners. So I conclude that these are separate paragraphs, with wealthy believers challenged in 4:13–17 and wealthy pagans condemned in 5:1–6.

CHRISTIAN MERCHANTS NEED DEPENDENCE ON GOD (4:13–17)

The Presumptuous Plans (4:13)

"Now listen, you" (*age nyn*) is a prophetic particle of disapproval telling these readers to wake up and open their ears to God and his warning. It returns to the polemic of 1:9–11; 2:5–7; and 4:1–3, denouncing serious sin in the community. It resembles Jesus' "Whoever has ears, let them hear" (Matt 11:15; 13:9, 43). James is picturing his readers as itinerant merchant traders who in the first century would have been what we today call "new money," a wealthy group of Jews whom Josephus said would stop at nothing to make more money (*Antiquities* 12.2–5; also Sirach 26:29).

James depicts them here as making plans for future business trips. Clearly God has been left out of the picture, as their deliberations are entirely self-centered: "Today or tomorrow we will go to this or that city, [we will] spend a year there, [we will] carry on business and [we will] make money." No God needed! They do not ask "if it is the Lord's will" (4:16) or say they will "go to this or that city, serve God, and carry on business." They think the world is their oyster, there for the taking, and they don't need any help from God. Time is irrelevant, since it exists only for their profit (note the implied repeated "we ... we ... we"). Everything is part of the plan, even the time limits (a year), and their assumption is that all that matters is making money and building an earthly kingdom (similar to the greedy exploitation of the situation in 2 Pet 2:3).

The sin is not in the planning or even in the desire for profit but in the boastful, self-engrossed attitude. The self is the total focus and God a forgotten footnote in their lives. Their blind disregard for eternal realities will have frightening consequence not just for the immediate future but for eternity. On the surface this seems completely normal for business plans, and the confidence of the merchants seems to make a lot of sense. This exact thing takes place every day in the lives of too many Christian businesspeople. These plans could stem from the *Wall Street Journal* or the boardrooms of a thousand corporations. The Romans conquered the world through their trade as much as through their armies, and these "rich Christians in an age of plenty" are going along for the ride.

THE TRUE PERSPECTIVE FOR BUSINESS (4:14–15)

The obvious problem is not in their plans per se but in the absence of God from their lives. The fact that the sovereign will of God is never considered in their plans is a huge error. Such presumption and a narcissistic preoccupation with self invites disaster of eternal proportions. Certainly profitable plans and business goals are perfectly fine if God is in the picture and in charge. For those called by God to a merchant career, making money is a valid part of the picture, but the purpose is to serve God and help others with that money, and such can be as much a "spiritual gift" as my call to teach the word of God.

God calls people to a life in the business world as clearly as he does to the pastorate or the mission field. However, both the source of the call and its goal are Godward, not pleasure-oriented. The purpose is the same in each case—glorifying God and not self and using our gift to serve God and his people. The point for businesspeople is clear: God wants to be their "senior partner," the CEO of their "ministry" in business. He demands to guide and direct their portfolio and plans. The goal is to pray about the plans as you are making them and to follow his leading. I spent a great deal of time in prayer when I changed from pastoring to teaching, as well as when returning to Trinity from Canada in my teaching, and when deciding to write every book I have produced. That is exactly what businesspeople should do regularly as they plan new business ventures.

Notice how James states verse 14: "Why, you do not even know what will happen tomorrow." "You" is *hoitines*, implying that "people like you" (titans of trade and industry), no matter how much earthly authority you wield, can only guess what the immediate future holds. You "know" nothing about the future. Contingency controls every plan, and the God of all contingencies must at all times direct such planning.

There is some question about the added "What is your life?" In the NIV, NRSV, and ESV it is a separate sentence and centers on the readers' present life, but in the NASB, HCSB, NLT, and LEB it is included as part of the preceding sentence and centers on the future: "How do you know what your life will be like tomorrow?" (NLT), following the UBS (Greek) text. It is a very difficult decision, as the two readings both fit well. However, I think the emphasis on present existence makes more sense here so will go with the two-sentence version as in the NIV.

James grounds this warning in the temporary nature of life itself. We are nothing but "a mist that appears for a little while and then vanishes." When I was in my twenties and thirties I did not truly understand this, but as I approach seventy-six (with my body telling me every day how much it dislikes me!), I know exactly what this is saying. Mist was a natural metaphor, since at the border of the Mediterranean the morning fog was a constant event. It appeared most mornings but lasted a very short time and then went away just like that. The brevity of life was a frequent emphasis (Job 7:7, 9; Pss 39:5–6; 103:15–16; Prov 27:1; Isa 40:6–7; Luke 12:16–20).

So James now tells all these merchants (and every one of us) what "you ought to say" whenever you make plans (4:15): "If it is the Lord's will, we will live and do this or that." We have no idea whether we will be alive tomorrow morning, so it is incumbent on us to consciously live under the Lord's will and quit trying to take charge of our lives. All planning must include "if the Lord wills," and it is amazing how greatly this reverberates through Scripture (Pss 40:8; 143:10; Isa 46:20; 53:10; Matt 6:10; Mark 3:35; Rom 12:2; 15:32; Heb 13:21; 1 Pet 3:17; 4:2). James's choice of "the Lord" is deliberate, stressing that God (probably including Christ) is Lord of the universe and in complete charge. Our hopes and desired plans must surrender to the guiding presence of the Godhead at all times.

I have a nephew who was in one of the buildings destroyed in the 9/11 terrorist attack and ran out after the first plane struck, getting onto a ferry. He watched the second plane do its U-turn and fly over his ferry on its way into the second building. His wife worked in one of the top floors and would have been killed if she had not that very day been enrolling one of their children in nursery school. Another nephew was a colonel who led many of the "first-responder" soldiers and was nearly killed by falling glass. Our lives are truly out of our control and entirely in God's hands. All our actions ("do this or that") must be placed in his hands. So in all of our detailed planning (which we need to do), we must pray for God's guidance and will, following the Gethsemane prayer (Mark 14:36), "yet not what I will, but what you will." Total surrender to God's providential will is the key to success.

BOASTING AND THE SIN OF OMISSION (4:16–17)

In these verses James makes absolutely clear where the problem lies—namely, in their arrogant assumption that they are in control and as a result "boast in your arrogant schemes." In itself, pride and boasting can be valid and positive, as the "boasting" of the poor and rich in 1:9–10. We are justly proud of the work of God in our lives and in our children's accomplishments. However, what is seen in these "worldly" businesspeople is sinful arrogance because it is self-pride that assumes it is in charge.

There are three ways to understand this sentence, depending on how you interpret the preposition *en*. It could tell how they are boasting—namely, "in" or "by" arrogant schemes (boasting proudly)—or it could provide content, telling that they are boasting "about" their arrogant schemes. It is also possible to see it as temporal—they are boasting "when" they arrogantly make their plans and leave God out of it. I personally would combine these latter two. This becomes a type of idolatry, for they are setting their own decisions above the will of God and basically worshipping themselves. No wonder James concludes, "All such boasting is evil." God is not just ignored; he is virtually held up in ridicule as irrelevant compared to the merchant's own desires and plans.

James then concludes in 4:17 with an early Christian creedal saying, which has come to be called "the sin of omission." He takes a basic theological truth about sin and applies it to the arrogant boasting and disregard of God on the part of these worldly Christian merchants. There is a good chance that he adds it here not just as a conclusion to this paragraph but as a general summary of all the "sins" of his letter thus far. It is certainly a very important reminder of a critical fact, that sin is not just in the deeds we commit but also in the deeds we should commit but fail to perform—that is, what you "ought to do" but don't do. Each of them (hearing without doing, discrimination, failing to aid the needy, backbiting and slander, leaving God out of decisions) we know well as being divine demands but in our self-centered worldliness ignore in our lives. We probably commit this sin even more regularly than overt sins.

This sin of omission is quite clear. It involves good deeds you are well aware you are required by God to perform regularly, especially here depending on God and yielding to his guidance and will in business decisions. This includes using our worldly resources to enhance the kingdom and help the needy among us. "Doesn't do it" is in the present tense and means that on a regular basis we refuse to do what God wants us to do. In other words, this is ongoing sin and will bring God's wrath down on our heads not just for the sins we commit but also for the good we should be doing and refuse to do in our hedonistic pursuit of personal pleasure.

Examples abound in Scripture, as in the servant who begs for forgiveness but refuses to forgive in Matthew 18:21–35, the rich ruler who refuses to yield his resources to God in Luke 18:18–30, or the failure of the self-centered disciples to cast the demon out of the child in Mark 9:14–19. The failure to help others when you have the resources to do so is a frequent "sin of omission" every one of us commits. Our pride in our earthly achievements and possessions all too often outweighs our commitment to God and his will. Our discretionary funds most of the time are used for self rather than for God or others. There is all too much in our lives for which we will have to answer to God!

UNGODLY LANDOWNERS
OPPRESS THE POOR (5:1–6)

WARNING OF JUDGMENT FOR HOARDING WEALTH (5:1–3A)

Now James turns his attention from wealthy believers to unbelievers, specifically to landowners who are oppressing their poor laborers and stealing their money by refusing to pay them a fair wage. He begins with the same prophetic particle of disapproval ("Now listen, you") with which he began 4:13–17. The rebuke of the earlier passage was much less stern than what we have here, for the sins—namely, the vicious mistreatment of others—are far more severe. We return to the issues of rich and poor in 1:9–11 and especially 2:1–13, for the wealthy visitors to the Christian "synagogues" in 2:2, 6–7, are also enemies of the church (as they are here).

So these are not believers like in 4:13–17, for the tone of the paragraph is consistently condemnation rather than challenge, and it follows Old Testament diatribe against wealthy oppressors. All encouragement is reserved for the victims, with little hope for the greedy rich. The Christian merchants of the previous passage ignored God in their plans, but these ungodly people have gone an extra step, cheating their poverty-stricken workers in order to have more money for their luxurious lifestyle. This passage contains no appeal to recognize God, for he has no place whatsoever in these wealthy pirates' lives. So there is only certain judgment awaiting them, starting with the disappearance of their wealth (5:3) and ending with their "slaughter" as fattened cattle ready for the sacrifice (5:5b).

This opening verse begins on a somber note, offering no repentance but calling on these oppressors only to "weep and wail because of the misery that is coming on you." The two verbs, *klaiō* and *ololyzō*, are onomatopoetic; they sound like the wailing they describe. They are often used in prophetic writings for the laments and grief of those condemned by God of serious sins (Isa 10:30; 13:6; 14:31; Ezek 21:12; Hos 7:14; Amos 5:16; Zech 11:2–3). Many of the passages center on the day of the Lord and final judgment, and that is the case here as well. In Luke 23:28 Jesus called on Jerusalem to "weep for yourselves and for your children," and in Revelation 18:11, 15, 19, the pagan kings, merchants, and ship captains who profited from the evil empire will "weep and mourn" in light of the absolute destruction that will soon overtake them.

These are evil landowners who out of avarice have stolen the property and wages of their workers. They controlled the markets, the movement of trade, and the banks. As a result, they would force the small independent farmers into bankruptcy, foreclose on them, and steal their property. They would turn them into tenant farmers and then pay them very little in order to get rich at their expense. So the God of justice is paying them back for the evil they have done. Note closely that Scripture passages like this are not condemning all who are rich but only those who have cheated to get rich and misused their wealth to live in luxury and refused to use it for the kingdom and to help others. I consider wealth one of the "spiritual gifts," given to those whom God wants to use to alleviate suffering in others. It is to be an *opportunity* for ministry, not just a means of living with a high lifestyle.

Their riches are pictured as already gathered and stored up for the pleasure of these people. These are perfect-tense verbs, stative in force; that is, they describe the current state of affairs. Some think of this as "prophetic anticipation"—that is, a future reference—but I follow those who see it as having an inaugurated thrust, depicting an evil process that has already begun and building into the future. It is stated generally (riches), and then James adduces specific examples (garments, gold and silver). The clothes describe luxurious garments that were highly sought after and were among the most precious possessions, even given as heirlooms to descendants. Gold and silver of course were the primary source of wealth then as now.

The idea of riches rotting is strange; while garments decay, gold and silver do not. However, in the ancient world this was a general image for what was temporary, and wealth like all earthly things fits that category perfectly. Just look at how long the riches of lottery winners typically last. I have read that the majority lose it all within a couple of years. How many of the richest families in the world in the nineteenth and early twentieth centuries still have their wealth? Like every aspect of our earthly existence, our wealth is doomed to disappear. This is especially true for those who have used their riches for evil purposes and have garnered it by immoral means. The idea of extravagant garments as moth-eaten is a common image (Job 13:28–14:2; Isa 50:9; 51:8; Matt 6:19–20). The picture is not just of disappearing but of a disgraceful, ignominious end.

The same sad end is reserved for the money, which has "corroded," or "rusted." Of course, the metals gold and silver don't rust, but this was a common metaphor for the fact that ill-gotten gain will never last and is doomed (Sirach 29:10; Baruch 6:11; Letter of Jeremiah 10). Since many metals do rust away, this has an "as if" flavor to it. Some think James speaks of this wealth as false or counterfeit coins because it has no worth with God. The same Greek term (*ios*) is used both for the poison of 3:8 and the rust here, speaking of a destructive potion that takes away a thing's very existence. The message is that what they trust the most to ensure their future (their earthly riches) will pass away and leave them with nothing.

Two further images drive home James's point: (1) These land-owners' wealth will "testify against" them, meaning it will stand as evidence of their wrongdoing at the final judgment. This legal proof will bring about a guilty verdict, resulting in eternal judgment for the evil they have done. They will not be able to hide the evidence of their hedonistic lifestyle, and it will prove to all the extent of their evil practices. (2) Their wealth will also prove their guilt, and it will result in a verdict of hellfire and brimstone. The picture is of the rust not only corroding but also eating away the metal. This image of fiery judgment occurs in Psalm 21:9 ("his fire will consume them") and Judith 16:17 ("fire will devour them"). In 1 Peter 1:6–7 this fire will "test" believers and prove them genuine, but it has the opposite effect on unbelievers. In Jesus' teaching the imagery of hell is built on Gehenna, the trash dump in the Hinnom Valley outside the walls of Jerusalem where the fires burnt 24/7 (Matt 5:22, 29–30; 10:28). In Revelation 19:20; 20:14–15; 21:8 it is the "lake of fire" where the wicked will spend eternity.

THE CRIES OF THE POOR (5:3B–4)

Sarcasm drips and produces a flood of invective, as their doomed "treasure" is accumulating and being stored up for the "last days." For God's people who are living for him, all that we sacrifice and surrender for him is immediately banked in heaven and will become eternal reward at the last judgment (Luke 16:8–9). On the other hand, the ungodly wealthy are "hoarding" all their riches for themselves but in reality are storing up for themselves judgment.

The stark contrast is devastating. For those sacrificing for God these will be days of vindication and eternal reward. For those living only for the riches of this world, they will prove the "last" of their wealth, for their eternity will be one of endless loss.

This is not just a future event but is what we call "inaugurated **eschatology**," meaning that the last days have begun already. The tension between the already and the not-yet is a critical truth. The unsaved have already brought divine judgment on themselves, but it has not yet been finalized. For a short time they will enjoy this world's plenty, but it will soon come to an end, and will do so with finality. That will come at the return of Christ and the events of the **eschaton**, or end of human history. They believe they are accumulating treasure for a luxury-laden retirement, but in actuality they are storing up wrath that will come with their eternal "retirement." We are living now in the last days and must be ready for eternity, not merely centered on the here and now. Being wealthy is not a sin, but using that wealth for self is.

James stresses the second sin (after hoarding their wealth) in 5:4—namely, cheating their workers from the wages they have earned. James is quite specific and powerful in his indictment: "Look," he tells us, understand the gravity of their wickedness. Building on the image of the blood of Abel crying out from the ground in Genesis 4:10, there is a double cry from the laborers in the field. First, the stolen wages cry out to God,[1] and then the harvesters themselves cry out for vindication and revenge. The "harvesters" were day laborers hired at harvest time to cut down the wheat and other grains to be picked. They have been defrauded

---

1. There is widespread disagreement about whether this should read "the wages you withheld" or "held back" (*aphysterēmenos*, NIV, NLT, NASB, NET, LEB) or "the wages you stole" or "kept back by fraud" (*apesterēmenos*, NRSV, ESV). While most versions opt for the former, the more widely attested verb (A B² Ψ) is the latter, so it is preferred by most commentators. James is saying they are nothing but common thieves.

of the wages they earned. Galilee had been bought up for the most part by wealthy absentee landlords, and the small farmers had been forced off their land and then made to hire themselves out to these very land barons who had stolen their land.

The problem of withholding pay from workers had been common for centuries, and the workers had little redress since these rich exploiters controlled the court system as well. Several passages show how old this practice was. Leviticus 19:13 says, "Do not defraud or rob your neighbor," and Deuteronomy 24:14-15 applies this to field workers: "Do not take advantage of a hired worker. ... Pay them their wages each day. ... Otherwise they may cry to the LORD against you" (see also Job 7:2; 31:38-40; Jer 22:13; Mal 3:5; Matt 20:1-16; Sirach 7:20; Tobit 4:14).

These cries are made both by the wages kept back and the workers themselves, highlighting the depth of the sin. Moreover, these are pleas for vengeance (as in Gen 18:20; Exod 2:23; 1 Sam 9:16; Ps 12:5). They have succeeded and have "reached the ears of the Lord Almighty." God's response is often recorded, as in Romans 12:19, "It is mine to avenge; I will repay" (cited from Deut 32:35). This promise is assumed by the martyrs in Revelation 6:10: "How long, sovereign Lord, holy and true, until you judge the inhabitants of the earth and avenge our blood?" In a very real sense the rest of the book of Revelation is a chronicle telling how God responds to their cry. This paragraph centers on his response to this cry—namely, with condemnation and judgment.

James's emphasis is on the identity of the One who hears and responds. He is "Lord Almighty," or as the NLT translates it, "the Lord of Heaven's Armies" (traditionally "the Lord of hosts," *kyrios Sabaōth*). The picture is of God as Lord of creation leading his angelic army in defense of his persecuted and cheated people (1 Sam 17:45; 2 Sam 6:18; Isa 1:24; 2:12; 6:3, 5; Jer 49:5, 7, 26). Justice will be meted out and his suffering people vindicated. Those who defraud the poor may get away with their evil deeds for now, but they will answer to God at the final judgment.

PREPARING THE RICH FOR THE SLAUGHTER (5:5-6)

James enumerates the third sin (after hoarding wealth and cheating workers) in 5:5: self-indulgent luxury. Once more, he is not condemning all who are wealthy, nor does he indict their work ethic. His invective is directed at their selfish, pleasure-driven lifestyle and their dishonesty in cheating their workers. As Jesus said in Luke 6:24, "But woe to you who are rich, for you have already received your comfort." In other words, they have lived for the earthly luxuries they could command and have no heavenly reward. Because they have even stolen the wages of their day laborers to feed their obsession for luxuries, they will receive only condemnation at God's *bēma*, or judgment seat.

As a result of their hedonistic indulgence, James tells them, "You have fattened yourselves in the day of slaughter." This depiction of judgment uses a powerful metaphor. In the ancient world those cattle who were to be slaughtered as sacrifices to God (or the gods) were allowed to graze all the time in order to fatten them up "for slaughter" (the common term for sacrifice) on the altar. So the wanton lifestyle of these "fat cats" depicts this earthly existence as a huge pastureland for these wealthy people.

Some see a different analogy here, depicting victorious warriors in a gluttonous feast after the victory. In this view the "day of slaughter" would not refer to the judgment day but to the "slaughter" (metaphorical) of the pious poor. Thus the wealthy would be gorging themselves on the lives of their workers and enjoying the process of defrauding them to the point that they starve to death. This has a certain validity to it and could well be correct. However, the imagery of the last judgment[2] is more likely than that of their wanton murder of their workers (that comes in v. 6 rather than here).

---

2. Some see this as more the AD 70 destruction of Jerusalem rather than the final judgment, but the context makes the latter the more probable view.

The literal phrase is "fattened your hearts" (*ethrepsate tas kardias hymōn*), a metaphor for indulgent gluttony as they moved closer and closer to the time of slaughter—namely, the day of judgment at the return of Christ. In Amos 4:1–2 the wealthy women who "oppress the poor" are called "the cows of Bashan" (an area east of the Jordan known for its well-fed cattle) who were being made ready for the exile. In Jeremiah 12:3 the enemies of God are described as "sheep to be butchered … set … apart for the day of slaughter." Again, there is an inaugurated thrust as the day of judgment is portrayed as already begun with their gluttonous practices. Some commentators see this as hyperbole and not really describing an actual situation, but I disagree. Such a picture was widespread then and is if anything even more so now.

The fourth and worst evil of them all occurs here, as James describes these rich sinners as having "condemned and murdered the innocent one, who was not opposing you." The fact that this is singular rather than plural is problematic, as some think it a reference to the trial and death of Jesus "the righteous one" (*ton dikaion*) or even of James himself (some who think this a pseudonymous work). However, the context makes this unlikely, and these must be the innocent Christian workers at the hands of the evil landowners. The purpose of the singular is to stress the fact that these misdeeds are directed against these workers one by one. There is no generality here.

The phrase "condemned and murdered" does not mean they are literally running them through with swords but rather that by their greedy actions they are condemning these workers to starve to death (see Ps 10:8–9; Amos 2:6; Mic 2:6–9; 6:9–16; 1 Enoch 95:7; 96:8) in order to feed their greed. This may also allude back to 2:6–7, where the wealthy were dragging poor believers into court and slandering the name of Jesus.

These righteous and innocent poor were not "opposing," or "resisting," these selfish manipulations. This nonresistance refers to the surrender of their lives and of the justice that was due them to God. They refuse to take matters into their own hands and fight back. As is said of Jesus in 1 Peter 2:23, "When they hurled their insults at him, he did not retaliate; when he suffered, he made no threats. Instead, he entrusted himself to him who judges justly." This does not mean the poor are not to protest and decry the evil deeds of the rich. The platform of Martin Luther King and those who took paths of nonresistance with him was exactly right as a protest against the evil of racial discrimination.

JAMES ENCOURAGES HIS CHURCHES TO SUFFER PATIENTLY (5:7-11)

Several scholars place 5:7-11 as the first paragraph of the conclusion to the book, and this is a possible reading, for it could culminate the whole letter and not just this closing section (4:13-5:6). However, it is so closely tied especially to 5:1-6 that I am following the majority, who see this as the counter to the evil actions of the wealthy landowners in 5:1-6. Still, this section provides a transition to the final conclusion and draws together several themes from the rest of the letter, as we will see. It provides a passage of comfort and encouragement following the devastating news regarding their immediate future at the hands of the rich oppressors.

Call for Patience (5:7-8)

James has just predicted very hard times for his poverty-stricken churches at the hands of the ungodly wealthy, so now he turns to his immediate readers and encourages them that the Lord has not forgotten them, and their reward is on the way. They must be willing to wait patiently for their coming victory to arrive. James adduces three models of patient endurance—the farmer (v. 7), the prophets (v. 9), and Job (v. 11)—all of whom learned to rely on God in times of trouble. In light of 5:1-6, the righteous learn not to retaliate (5:6b) but instead to let God take over.

He returns to addressing them as family ("brothers and sisters," fourteen times thus far) as part of that encouragement, reminding them that God takes care of his own. "Then" (*oun*) provides an inference from the wicked oppression of the righteous innocent in 5:6. They are challenged to remember that God will vindicate his people and punish their enemies and thus calls on them to persevere "until the Lord's coming." The ungodly rich will continue to flourish in this sin-laden world, but their time will soon end when Christ returns as conqueror.

The verb *makrothymeō*, which means both "be patient" and "wait," occurs four times in verses 7–10. They are to bear up in the hard times and trust God to end it all in his time. This combines passive waiting with an active trust in the Triune Godhead. They are not to seek active vengeance but rather allow God to avenge them, as in Romans 12:19: "Do not take revenge ... but leave room for God's wrath, for it is written: 'It is mine to avenge; I will repay.'" The payback is left to God, for his future action is 100 percent certain. Christ's "return" (*parousia*) pictures the arrival of a king on his war horse to deliver his people and return this world to its Creator (Matt 24:3, 27, 37, 39; 1 Cor 15:23; 1 Thess 4:15; 2 Thess 2:1–2, 8). The "Lord" is Jesus, the conquering King, Judge of the enemies of God, and vindicator of the righteous.

His first example of this patient waiting is the farmer who "waits for the land to yield its valuable crop, patiently waiting for the autumn and spring rains." This image provides a perfect illustration, for all they can do is plant, weed, and wait for the crops to arrive. He asks them to "see," or "consider carefully" (*idou*), the necessity of waiting for the harvest like a farmer. Farming was among the most important occupations in Palestine, and Jesus was constantly using agricultural images in parables and illustrations. The crop was "valuable" or "precious" (*timion*) like jewels because it determined whether the people would have food and live for another year.

The "autumn and spring rains" are literally "the early and late rains," a weather feature of the Mediterranean climate mentioned often in Scripture (Deut 11:14; Jer 5:24; Hos 6:3; Joel 2:23; Zech 10:1).

Autumn was the time for planting and spring the time for har-vesting. They signified God's mercy and faithfulness in taking care of his people, and all the farmer could do was wait for these rains to arrive. The parallels are quite close. The ancient farmer, like us, had no control over the events of this world. For him it was weather disasters or crop failure. For us it is the contingent events of history. We like the farmer can only be patient and trust God to watch over us and bring the promised harvest, which for us is a harvest of souls at the eschaton, or end of history, when Christ comes.

James makes this point clear in verse 8: "You too, be patient and stand firm, because the Lord's coming is near." "Stand firm" in Greek is literally "strengthen your hearts" (*stērixate tas kar-dias hymōn*). While the rich are "fattening their hearts" (5:5), the faithful are strengthening theirs in hope and trust in their Lord. The righteous surrender to God, rely on him, and are empowered by the Holy Spirit in this evil world, and that is why they can be patient; they know he will fulfill his promises. God's people are resolute in the face of adversity, committed to God and his control of this world. The wicked may prosper for a time, but "the Lord is near," and their age will soon be over.

So interestingly, "strength" in this instance means waiting, but it is an active rather than passive waiting, an energy-laden trust in God that enables us to persevere in the midst of rampant evil. Paul tells the Roman believers that he wants to "impart to you some spiritual gift to make you strong" (Rom 1:11), and Peter states that "after you have suffered a little while," God "will himself restore you and make you strong, firm and steadfast" (1 Pet 5:10). What these readers (and we) need is to find an inner strength by waiting with a firm trust in the Lord. As the pagan wealthy turn to their riches and hedonistic pleasures, God's people find the strength and courage to turn to God and wait patiently for him to act.

We all must admit that we have difficulties with the "soon" here. It has now been more than two thousand years since this promise was uttered, and it seems evil has been the force getting stronger of late. Part of the kingdom message in Mark 1:14–15, and one of the major stresses of Scripture, is that "the kingdom of God has come near." The imminence of the **parousia** is mentioned often in the Gospels (Matt 3:2; 4:17; 10:7; 24:32–33; Luke 10:9, 11), in Paul (Rom 13:12; 1 Cor 16:22), in the General Letters (Heb 10:25, 37; 1 Pet 4:7), and in Revelation (1:3; 3:11; 22:7, 12, 20).

Yet the "soon" return seems no closer than it did two millennia ago. The normal answer is 2 Peter 3:8 ("With the Lord a day is like a thousand years, and a thousand years are like a day") and 9 ("The Lord … is patient with you, not wanting anyone to perish, but everyone to come to repentance"). Our God is timeless, and we must see the "near return" according to his idea of time rather than ours. Jesus himself did not know how long his return would take (Mark 13:32), and that is a large part of the "waiting." Finally, there is an inaugurated aspect in that we are now living in the last days, experiencing the tension between the "already" and the "not yet." Christ can return at any time, and so we live and conduct ourselves within that promise.

Avoiding Dissension (5:9)

Since the Lord's return is near, final judgment is around the corner. That is all the more reason to avoid sin, for James's readers will have to answer for it very soon. So he returns to the serious problem of 4:1–10 that has so endangered his churches and provides a further reason to avoid the conflicts that were splitting them. The pressure on them from their mistreatment at the hands of the wicked landowners was producing discouraged and tension-filled believers who were starting to lash out and "grumble against one another." The verb stenazō is used of "groaning" and "complaining" and recalls the wilderness wanderings of the Israelites. But in that case they were complaining about God and Moses, while here they are grumbling about each other.

The principle recalls Matthew 7:1: "Do not judge, or you too will be judged." If they are allowing their anger to get the best of them and are turning against each other, they will face an angry God. They are "brothers and sisters," members of the family of God, and love and peace should characterize their community. The principle of biblical ethics is clear: what you do to others you are doing to God, for they are made in his image, and your actions will come back on you (whether good or bad; see also 2:13; 4:11–12).

The last part of this verse combines 4:12 ("one Lawgiver and Judge") with 5:8 ("the Lord's coming is near"). "The Judge is standing at the door" means that judgment is imminent, and grumblers won't get away with a thing. There is some debate regarding whether "the Judge" refers to God or specifically to Christ, but James could have both in mind (= the Triune Godhead), for at the great white throne they will judge together.

This call is an eschatological statement similar to Mark 13:29 ("when you see these things happening, you know that it is near, right at the door") and Revelation 3:20 ("Here I am! I stand at the door and knock"). "Door" is plural "doors" (*tōn thyrōn*) and is more than an idiom for "soon." The doors are the gates of heaven, with the imagery of the open heaven (at Jesus' baptism in Mark 10 and parallels; at the revelation of heaven to John in Rev 4:1; also Acts 7:56; 10:11; 2 Cor 12:1–4). Here it is heaven's courtroom, and again it has an inaugurated force, as the judgment is beginning and will consummate at the great white throne of Revelation 20:11–15.

SECOND CALL FOR PATIENT SUFFERING (5:10–11)

As in verses 7–8, James challenges the readers to suffer for Christ with patient endurance, adducing two more examples: the prophets and Job. James is explicit here, saying "as an example … take" and using *hypodeigma*, a "pattern, model" that the readers can emulate. This is similar to the "roll call of heroes" in Hebrews 11, which presents a series of models from the Old Testament for the readers to follow. In both cases the **typological** examples portray patient endurance in the midst of hard times. The prophets are especially prominent in Hebrews 11:33–38, where they "through faith conquered kingdoms ... shut the mouths of lions, quenched the fury of the flames ... whose weakness was turned to strength ... who were tortured, refusing to be released so that they might gain an even better resurrection. ... They were put to death by stoning; they were sawed in two; they were killed by the sword."

The means by which they accomplished this was the "patient suffering" and perseverance noted three times in 5:7–8 and twice more here. The prophets suffered especially because they "spoke in the name of the Lord," which some interpret as a cry against injustice, but it is broader here and includes the call to repentance and getting right with God. As in John 3:19–20, darkness hates light and tries to extinguish it, and so the prophets were models for all Christian suffering, bearing up the hatred and oppression of the world to glorify God and Christ.

As the Jews did for generations, followed by the Christians, God's people ever since have "called blessed"—*makarizomen*, like in the beatitudes of Matthew 5 (*makarios*)—"those who have persevered" (5:11). This should not be mistranslated as "happy" or "fortunate" (as in TLB, REB, TEV), for those being persecuted are never happy (Heb 12:11, "no discipline seems pleasant at the time, but painful"). Rather it means that those who suffer for Christ are blessed by God in a special way (see earlier on 1:2). In 1:12, the particular blessing for such endurance was "the crown of life"; here it is divine blessing in general.

The second model for endurance is Job, whose trust in God led to incredible perseverance in the light of systemic suffering. This builds on verse 10, where the prophets exemplified patience or longsuffering (*makrothymia*), while here Job builds on this and exemplifies the perseverance (*hypomonē*) that results. The two obviously function together to describe the proper Christian reaction to suffering—namely, an attitude of longsuffering that expresses itself in endurance of evil.

At first glance Job does not seem a model of patience, for he often complained bitterly, asking God why he had to go through all the suffering (Job 7:11-21; 10:18-22; 13:20-27; 23:2-7; 30:20-23). Few Jewish writings used Job as an example, with the exception of the Testament of Job. James may have been aware of it or the tradition behind it, for that work often extolled Job's patient endurance (Testament of Job 1:5; 25:4-5; 27:6-7). Still, in the biblical book of Job he never denounced either God or his faith in God and remained faithful to the end, as in the concluding 42:2 ("I know that you can do all things; no purpose of yours can be thwarted"), and in 42:7 the Lord commends Job for having "spoken the truth about me." So in reality Job was indeed a model of patient faithfulness to God.

James stresses both hearing and seeing: "You have heard of Job's perseverance and have seen what the Lord finally brought about." He expects his readers to be fully aware of the lesson Job had for them and to apply it to their own lives. "Seen what the Lord finally brought about" is literally "seen the end [*telos*] of the Lord"; *telos* can mean either "end" or "purpose." It could refer to the end of what God "*finally* brought about" or "the outcome" in restoring his fortune (NIV, REB, NLT, LEB, HCSB) or to the purpose or goal that the events produced in Job's life (NASB, NRSV, ESV, NET). Both options are quite viable and would fit well. Perhaps the "end" or "outcome" is slightly better, as it fits Job (42:5-6) and the New Testament tradition, as in Matthew 10:22: "the one who stands firm to the end will be saved" (also 1 Cor 1:8; Heb 3:14).

In the epilogue of Job (42:7-17), he received twice as much from the Lord as he had before. The lesson is that God rewards those who trust him and remain faithful through misfortune and suffering. We should take note of the message in Romans 8:26-28. When serious trials bombard us, we don't know how to pray as we should (8:26a) and can only endure with patient perseverance (Jas 5:7-8, 10-11). Yet we do know three things: The Spirit is praying for us more deeply than we are praying for ourselves

(Rom 8:26b); he is interceding for us and knows the mind of God (Rom 8:27); and for that reason God "causes everything to work together for the good of those who love God" (Rom 8:28 NLT).

Job's lesson is meant for us—namely, that "the Lord is full of compassion and mercy," an allusion to Psalm 103:8: "The LORD is compassionate and gracious ... abounding in love." His mercy is exercised on our behalf not just in spite of our suffering but because of it. He turns the painful experience (Heb 12:11a) into a "harvest of righteousness" (Heb 12:11b). As we patiently endure, we become "mature and complete, not lacking anything" (Jas 1:2–4). As God turns everything around for us, his "compassionate mercy" becomes all the more evident, and we grow stronger and stronger.

———

This is a very important section for the Western church in the twenty-first century; we have lived with systemic wealth for so long that we take it for granted. The only question for most of us is how much wealth we can generate for ourselves, not what we should do with it when we attain it. What a century ago would have constituted an incredible standard of living is today considered basic. The lessons of James 4:13–5:11 are very important for the church today, for the problems have been magnified in our times. One could say that wealth has become a tool of Satan as never before, tempting people to live for ourselves because it is so available to us.

The situation James describes in verses 13–17 is especially applicable to us, for in our consumer society we all tend to leave God out of our decisions. Our life unfolds not on the basis of what God wants us to do with our time and money but on the basis of what is convenient and what pleases us, forgetting God's place in our lives. Our focus is on how to make lots of money and how to spend what we have received. Studies have shown that at best the average Christian gives 2–3 percent back to the Lord and to help others.[3] Like the merchants here, we must learn our lives are fleeting (v. 14), and that this secular lifestyle will bear no fruit for eternity. We must center our decisions on living life according to God's will (v. 15) rather than on arrogant, self-centered boasting (v. 16). Moreover, these are sins of omission (v. 17), for we are well aware of what God wants of us but ignore eternal realities in favor of temporary pleasures.

In the next section (5:1–6) James addresses the ungodly rich who are stealing from their workers by refusing to pay the wages due them and who then use that money to implement their luxurious lifestyle. In our society many wealthy Christians have joined the pagans by becoming reverse Robin Hoods and "stealing from the poor and giving to the rich"—namely, themselves. The indictment here is meant for Christians as well as non-Christians in our day, for greed has become an addiction; all of us have "hoarded wealth in the last days" (v. 3) for our own selfish pleasures. We must ask ourselves how much evidence is gathering against us regarding our use of this world's resources for ourselves. The judgment is serious and totally frightening, for we will pay for our self-indulgent way of living (v. 5). God is just, and condemnation is certain for carnal Christians as well as non-Christians.

James's advice to the suffering poor in verses 7–11 is quite simple: wait patiently for God's justice to arrive. His promises are absolutely certain, but they will arrive at Christ's return as conquering King (v. 7). He then gives three examples of patient endurance—the farmer waiting for his harvest (v. 7), prophets waiting for their prophecies to take place (v. 10), and Job waiting for his vindication to arrive (v. 11). God's suffering people are guaranteed an eternal harvest, but in the meantime they must endure and persevere, trusting God to bring an end to evil in his own time.

---

3. Brian Dodd, "Generous Church: Ten Top Characteristics," *Church Leaders*, May 31, 2011, https://churchleaders.com/pastors/pastor-how-to/151049-brian-dodd-generous-church-ten-top-characteristics.html.

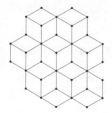

CONCLUDING EXHORTATIONS
(5:12–20)

At first glance this final section seems composed of three iso-lated and unrelated comments just thrown together in hap-hazard fashion. However, each is concerned with issues of speech (oaths, prayer, rescuing the fallen), and it is far more likely that James is presenting three final areas of need to his churches. These then become three areas of ministry critical to the life of the church. They are not just separate issues saved for last but rather a final set of examples of proper speech in the church address-ing critical needs.

James does not conclude like the other letters in the New Testament, with greetings, news about travel plans and situations at other churches, closing benedictions, or final farewells. Rather, he provides closing illustrations of the issues he has been speaking about throughout his letter. As in the case of the opening words of this letter, the ethical problems are so severe that he bypasses the normal closing to address the church directly on these issues.

SHALLOW OATHS ARE PROHIBITED (5:12)

Many scholars believe 5:12 functions at the section level, climax-ing 4:13–5:11, and that is viable. However, it may fit better with the concluding part of the book, as we will see below. This continues the emphasis on the misuse of speech and tells one major area where things can begin to turn around for the community, beginning the close of the letter.

As such, this is a transition verse, part of the series of negative commands (with 4:11; 5:9) on how the tongue should not be used in the community. At the same time, it also has a positive thrust, beginning the three exhortations of 5:12, 13–18, 19–20, that define the church as a corporate messianic community. Relating to both the admonitions of 4:13–5:11 and the concluding exhortations of 5:13–20, it brings together what precedes and what follows into a larger unity.

"Above all" seems to indicate that the making of vows is the most important issue in the letter, but that surely cannot be—the issues of enduring trials, practicing what you believe, treating the poor properly, and using the tongue to glorify God are hardly less important. So "above all" is a literary marker, and means something like "finally," indicating the concluding issues (like Paul in 2 Cor 13:11; Phil 4:8; 1 Thess 4:1).

People in the ancient world, when they wished to affirm a statement in a solemn manner, would invoke the gods, often adding, "May he strike me dead if this is not true." For the Jews God became a virtual legal witness to the veracity of the claim. It was so important that the Talmud devoted an entire tractate to it (Shebu'ot) with all sorts of distinctions between various kinds of oaths and statements on what was valid. By Jesus' time this had led to frivolous oaths that replaced honesty and truth. Jesus prohibited oaths in Matthew 5:33–37, but it is critical to recognize that he didn't mean all oaths whatsoever. God makes oaths (Heb 7:20–22, 28), as does Paul (Rom 1:9; 2 Cor 1:23; Gal 1:20). Jesus and James here were negating casual, shallow oath-taking.

James demands, "do not swear—not by heaven or by earth or by anything else." This echoes Jesus' admonition in Matthew 5:33–37, where he specifically mentions vows made by heaven, by earth, by Jerusalem, and by one's own head. Jesus' point was that we should stand by our own claims and be honest in our pronouncements rather than artificially base them on other authorities and then play fast and loose with our promises. This then became the basis for similar prohibitions elsewhere (2 Cor 1:17–18 and here). The stress in each instance is on personal honesty and integrity of speech.

The Old Testament frequently addresses the issue of oath-taking (Exod 20:7; Lev 19:12; Num 30:2; Deut 23:21–23). The purpose of vows was always to anchor the truthfulness of a statement, and even God took oaths to guarantee his promises and future actions in both testaments (Num 14:23; Deut 1:34; Ps 95:11; Heb 3:11; 4:3; 6:13; 7:20–22, 28). The Old Testament didn't so much prohibit oaths as demand integrity in keeping them. To break an oath was to profane the name of God (Lev 19:12). But by the time of Jesus and James, people made vows all the time, often with little intention of keeping them.

So in light of these insincere oaths both Jesus in Matthew 5:37 and James draw on Leviticus 19:12: "Do not swear falsely by my name and so profane the name of your God. I am the Lord." James thus commands that "a simple 'Yes' or 'No'" should more than suffice. All believers must be trustworthy and stand by their word. There should never be a need for an artificial oath to supplement the dependency of their promises. In all these texts breaking oaths is seen as insincerity and hypocrisy. A person's words should stand on their own, and half-truths should never be uttered.

Finally, the reader is warned that falling into such error will lead us to "be condemned," referring to both judgment via God's displeasure now and at the last judgment (as in 2:13; 5:9). Clearly, this is far more than a mere mistake. It is a sin against God, for he demands that his people be known for keeping their word. Integrity is absolutely essential, and so to hide shallow promises behind artificial oaths is a moral sin and not just a lapse in judgment.

Solemn oaths in court are not in view here, though the Essenes (the group at **Qumran**) thought so. They forbade oaths in general, while traditional Judaism cautioned them but allowed them when used expeditiously. The Anabaptist position against oath-taking in general and even in court situations is hard to justify in the New Testament and early church. Here and in the rest of the passages the message is standing by your word and keeping your promises.

JAMES CONNECTS PRAYER AND HEALING (5:13-18)

New Testament letters tend to end with a benediction or prayer for health and well-being, and this passage functions in that way. True, this is not a closing benediction and is not related to any earlier material in the letter, but James may have thought of this because prayer normally closed letters. He had already determined that the needs in his churches were so great that he would dispose of the normal traditional opening and closing format to emphasize the seriousness of the situation. Still, this and verses 19-20 substituted for those themes.

There is some relationship between 5:12 and 13. In 5:12 the speech problem is oath-taking; in 5:13 the speech answer is prayer. (In 1:5 it is prayer for wisdom.) Prayer is the central theme here. We surrender everything to God and rely on him for strength and wisdom. The progression of the prayer is first hierarchical (centering on the leaders in the community, 5:14), then corporate (5:14–15), and finally individual (5:16–18).

The passage progresses via four steps: The need for prayer and praise as basic responses to life's dilemmas (v. 13); the response to illness via prayer and anointing with oil (vv. 14–15a); the response to sin via confession (15b–16a); the power of righteous prayer to make a difference, using Elijah as the model (16b–18).

PRAYER AND PRAISE (5:13)

James has summed up all of life's experience in the simplest way possible—suffering and trouble on the one hand and happy occasions on the other. "Suffering ill" (*kakopathei*) here is another term for the trials of life (1:2–4) and definitely draws us back to that material, forming an **inclusio**, especially when there too the proper response is prayer (1:5). The verb is the cognate of the noun for the suffering of the prophets in 5:10 and means to "suffer misfortune," connoting the huge effort needed to withstand it. Both the difficulties of life and the perseverance needed to overcome them are part of its meaning.

The only viable response is to "pray," the basic verb for turning to God, used eighty-five times in the New Testament. It includes both leaving the situation in God's hands (the petitionary aspect) and seeking the Lord in times of trouble (the worship aspect). Both at the corporate and the individual levels, we can only respond to life's little surprises by renewing regularly our complete submission to the Lord. We need to feel his compassion and support when everything seems to go sideways and we seem to be all alone in an alien world. We must remember that prayer is active, not passive. We aren't sitting back in our rocking chair, hoping that God will finally get busy and solve the crisis for us, but are in the front lines of our lives, asking him for strength to persevere and wisdom to find answers.

When everything is going well, and we face the "happy" circumstance of a life of plenty, there is serious danger of falling into complacency and a narcissistic demand for more, as if we deserve only the good things of life. "Happy" (*euthymei*) refers to an inner joy and cheerfulness of heart. It can also be used of "taking courage" (Acts 27:22, 25) when things go wrong, but in this context the thrust is especially good health.

In this situation, it is best to "sing songs of praise," or psalms (*psalletō*). This is critically important because it makes us constantly aware that God is in control and watching over us. We dare not become proud and complacent in times of prosperity, like the church in Laodicea (Rev 3:17-18) that boasted, "I am rich; I have acquired wealth and do not need a thing." Christ retorted that in actuality they were "wretched, pitiful, poor, blind and naked." We can fall into this same trap, like the merchants of 4:13-16, who

experienced God's extreme displeasure. By singing God's praises
we remind ourselves that all the good in life comes as a gift from
him (1:17). We thank him for present blessings and trust him for
the future.

PRAYER AND ANOINTING WITH OIL (5:14–15A)

A third situation arises in 5:14, forming another ABA pattern,
with A = troublesome trials (13a, 14a) and B = happy times (13b).
The first referred to general suffering, this second to a specific
type: illness. "Weakness" (*astheneō*) can come in many forms—
weak faith (Rom 4:19; 8:26), weak human nature (Rom 5:6; 6:19),
timidity (1 Cor 2:3), weak conscience (1 Cor 8:11–12)—but here, as
many other places, it refers to weak health (Matt 8:17; Mark 8:56;
Luke 4:40; 5:15; Gal 4:13; 1 Tim 5:23). James may be referring to
a specific situation, and if so probably a serious illness. The
person appears helpless and bedridden, with the Greek *kamnonta*
(NIV: "sick person") literally meaning someone who is "worn out,
exhausted" (5:15). The elders pray "over" the person, expressing a holistic understanding of illness in the community, with
the physical, social, and spiritual aspects all integrated. Prayer
becomes the unifying mechanism that brings all together behind
the unfortunate individual.

The elders in Judaism were the heads of families and clans
who led the people in their daily lives (Exod 3:16, 18; Num 11:16–17).
In Jesus' day a council of seven elders directed civic life, and the
rulers of synagogues were usually chosen from among them. Thus
they directed both the civil and religious spheres of village life.
They also formed an important group in the Sanhedrin along with
the Sadducees and Pharisees (Matt 16:21; 26:3, 57, 59). The early
church tended to follow Jewish precedent in worship but also in
leadership, calling the heads of house churches "elders" as well as
"pastors" and "overseers." In Acts they led the church (Acts 11:30;
14:23; 15:2, 6; 16:4; 20:17; 21:18). In Acts and the Pastoral Letters
the three metaphors (elder, pastor, overseer) refer to the same

office and provide interrelated pictures of the responsibility of the church leaders.

The "elders" here are those with pastoral oversight, guardians of the flock. It is not that they have more prayer power but that they had spiritual authority and were known for their piety. It is natural to call on mature spiritual leaders in time of distress, for "the prayer of a righteous person is powerful and effective" (5:16).

Two aspects of the prayers are worthy of note. First, they pray "over" the sick (*ep auton*), the only place this is stated in the New Testament. Some think it refers to an exorcism or to exercising the gift of healing, but neither fits the language here. It may be best to think of it as simply referring to prayer "over" one confined to bed or perhaps the laying on of hands (Matt 19:13).

Second, the elders are to "anoint them with oil in the name of the Lord." There are three possibilities for the meaning of this anointing:

1. Medicinal: olive oil was a primary medicine in the ancient world, so they would have used the olive oil as an unguent to cure the disease while they prayed (Isa 1:6: "cleansed or bandaged or soothed with olive oil"; also Luke 10:34). Ancients believed it was useful for all kinds of ailments, so this is a very possible understanding. One difficulty is the command to do it "in the name of the Lord," so a medicinal meaning doesn't sound like the primary thrust for James.

2. Sacramental: The combination of oil and prayer developed into the *euchalaion* (*euchē*, "prayer" + *elaion*, "oil") for both spiritual and physical healing. Later, the Roman Catholic Church developed out of this the sacrament of "extreme unction," the anointing of those dying so their sins can be forgiven. However, the purpose here is to heal the sick, not penance for the dying. There may be a slight sacramental thrust in bringing the sacred presence and power of God into the situation, but no more than this.

3. Symbolic: This is the most probable function. At times Jesus and the disciples anointed people (Mark 6:13); at other times they did not do so (Mark 6:5). Anointing in Scripture connoted consecration to the Lord, and in this act the sick person is consecrated and set apart to God (like priests and kings in the Old Testament). The combination of the olive oil and the prayer channels the divine presence into the sick person's life, and the compassionate, healing Father in all his *chesed* (lovingkindness) and *emet* (faithfulness) is experienced at a deeper level.

The prayer and anointing are done "in the name of the Lord," as God is glorified and guides the entire process. The power of the name is stressed in Acts 3–4, where Peter heals the lame man "in the name" (Acts 3:6) and then tells the crowd the miracle took place on the basis of "Jesus' name and the faith that comes through him" (Acts 3:16, also 4:10). It is the name of Jesus that heals, and it is to his name that we bring glory in healing.

We must conclude that anointing is not required for healing, but it is a commendable practice (especially for serious illnesses) for its symbolic value and because it enables us to focus our prayers more thoroughly. I would recommend fasting along with it, as it symbolizes the surrender of life's necessities in order to worship God and depend only on him. The three—prayer, fasting, anointing with oil—call God's people into ever more serious reliance on the Lord and his loving, healing presence. These are all valuable, even essential, tools of spiritual surrender on the part of God's community to his will.

James next (5:15) makes a startling promise: "And the prayer offered in faith will make the sick person well; the Lord will raise them up." The word for "heal, make well" is *sōzō*, in this case meaning to "save physically," but it is also the basic term in Scripture for spiritual "salvation." Often this means the person was touched by God both physically and spiritually (Matt 9:21–22; Mark 5:28, 34; 10:52).

Primarily, the physical side is stressed here, but "in faith" brings in the spiritual side as well. When "raised up" is added, this undoubtedly means raised from the sickbed and returned to health. This encourages a new boldness in prayer, expecting God's healing presence in a new way.

However, should this expectation evolve into a virtual certitude that God must heal whenever the "prayer of faith" takes place? We must answer with the words of Paul: "Not at all!" (Rom 3:4, 6, 31; 6:2, 15). The faith in this instance is mainly that of the elders, but the sick person obviously shares their faith in the Lord. There is no emphasis here on a charismatic gift on the part of the elders; rather the stress is on their complete trust in God. God's loving care is uppermost. Mark 11:24 states, "Whatever you ask for in prayer, believe that you have received it, and it will be yours."

It is critical to realize that this does not lead to what is called "prosperity preaching," the belief that we can get completely healthy and wealthy just by asking God for it. This perspective is quite dangerous, even heretical, for it assumes that we control God simply by having faith and can command him to give us whatever we wish. God is sovereign, not us, and one of his necessary answers to prayer must often be no. Faith without doubting (1:5–8) is in God, not in our ability to get what we want from him. Prayer does indeed have incredible power to do wondrous things, but God alone decides when and how. Prosperity theology is a heresy. God dare not be made our lackey, captive to whatever whim we desire.

Still, does prayer change things? I believe it does, for it channels God's presence into situations, and as in 5:16 below it is "powerful and effective." When the entire community and others agree and pray, things get done that would not otherwise. The actual working of prayer and faith and its relationship with the sovereignty of God remains a mystery, but all of Scripture agrees that prayer makes a difference, and I leave the final decision at all times with him and address him from the perspective of the Gethsemane prayer, "not my will but yours be done" (Matt 26:39).

Finally, Romans 8:26 says, "We do not know what we ought to pray for"—that is, how to pray according to the will of God—"but the Spirit himself intercedes for us" and "intercedes for God's people in accordance with the will of God." Therefore, "in all things God works for the good of those who love him" (Rom 8:28). This means that in many instances God will have to say "no" or "wait" because it is not in our best interest to give us what we are asking for. So the no when we are asking for healing is in reality a healing response, and we need the faith to accept that. The result will *always* be what is best for us. These will be times when saying no to physical healing actually brings about spiritual healing.

Still, the prayer of faith does carry with it the positive expectation that God will respond, and his healing presence will be felt. He will decide whether it will include physical or spiritual healing, or both. But the one thing that will always take place is growth in him and a sense of security, provided that we are centered on him in the situation.

SIN AND CONFESSION (5:15B–16A)

We are finite creatures who are continuously in need of spiritual healing and forgiveness. "If they have sinned" is a third-class condition (*kan* = *kai ean*) which assumes the possibility that sin lies behind the suffering and needs forgiveness (Mark 2:11–12; 1 Cor 11:27–30). To be sure, that is often not the case (John 9:3; 11:4; 2 Cor 12:8–10), but still, forgiveness is always needed by normal human beings. James intends here both general sins that occur in a person's life and specific sins that have led to the illness. As was the case in Jesus' healing ministry, God is at work both physically and spiritually, and those healed often get right with God in the process.

The corporate aspect is the subject of verse 16, as the people of God's community, the church, "confess your sins to each other and pray for each other," with the plural verbs and the *allēlois* standing for the members of the body of Christ. James adds "so that you may be healed" to indicate that sins lying behind the illness are certainly part of the picture. The term for "healed" (*iaomai*) nearly always relates to physical healing (Matt 5:8; 15:8; Luke 6:18; John 4:47; Acts 9:34), and this means that the spiritual state of the congregation as a whole is a factor in the healing presence of God. When there is serious sin in the individual (5:15) or the congregation (5:16), the prayers for healing are hindered in their effectiveness (1 Pet 3:7).

The confession is two-directional, as we open ourselves up both to God and to each other. Some read this verse as commanding confession only for those sins that have led to the illness, but I find that doubtful. James is speaking in a far more general way about the spiritual health of the congregation as a whole, as I have just said. We in God's messianic community are responsible for the health of the whole and for each other. As Acts 2:42, 44, says, "fellowship" is one of the pillars on which the church rests, and we must look out for one another spiritually. The Greek verb for "confess" means to "agree" as a group to a promise or declaration of truth and was often used in legal contexts for treaties or binding oaths. In the church community, it refers to a declaration of wrongdoing linked to a promise to stop committing that sin. All these aspects— the confession, the repentance, and the promise—are intended here (compare 1 John 1:9). Confession turns half-hearted prayer into "powerful and effective" prayer (5:16b).

It matters how God's people live, and when their relationship with God is hindered by sin, the power of their prayers is affected as well. We should not restrict the application of this verse to those sins that have caused the illness. James intends this generally. If we who are in need of prayer are part of a dynamic church, we experience God's presence and power in a new and vital way.

The Power of Righteous Prayer (5:16b–18)

True confession results in productive prayer. When the saints are walking with the Lord and centered on him, their prayers reflect that and accomplish great things. The truth is, "the prayer of a righteous person is powerful and effective." James mentions three different verbs for prayer in 5:13–18, *proseuchē* (six times), *euchē* (vv. 15, 16), and *deēsis* (v. 16). These are mostly synonymous (the latter two add the idea of intercession) and together connote the richness of prayer as placing our needs in God's hands. In one sense, every believer is a "righteous person," but James has in mind those saints who have confessed, received forgiveness (v. 15), and are walking closely with the Lord. All believers can and should pray, but those who are truly right with him and relying deeply on him have a special prayer power.

James identifies two effects of such prayers: they "have great power" (NLT) to do wondrous things in the lives of individuals and the church as a whole. Then also prayer has miraculous results, with the participle *energoumenē* either passive ("it is made effective" by the Spirit) or middle ("as it works"), with the latter perhaps more likely, since the power of prayer to do great things is uppermost. I would see it as producing virtually another main clause, "and produces wonderful results." Prayer changes things, and the spiritual maturity of both the individual and the congregation makes a huge difference.

As his model of a "righteous" individual and his prayers, James turns to Elijah (5:17), but he wants all his readers to realize that Elijah was not a superhero prayer warrior who is far above us but was "a human being, even as we are." Certainly he was the great miracle worker among the prophets, but he and Elisha had the same weaknesses and failures as the rest of us. A perusal of his story in 1 Kings 17–19 demonstrates this well. He prophesies a three-and-a-half-year famine and destroys 450 priests of Baal on Mount Carmel, but as soon as Queen Jezebel threatens him he runs for his life in panic and sits in complete dejection under a broom bush in the wilderness. What happened to the powerful prophet-warrior? He has become human like the rest of us and collapsed with the first sign of serious opposition.

Even when Elijah went from being a powerful prophet to being fearful and depressed, his prayers were still powerful and incredibly effective. James illustrates this with the prediction of 1 Kings 17–18, the lengthy drought in judgment of Ahab and the nation for turning to other gods. Two problems arise with James's account of Elijah:

1. First Kings 17:1 does not mention that Elijah "prayed earnestly" but rather that he prophesied from God. However, 1 Kings 18:42 tells us he prayed for the drought to end, and likely he prayed both before and after the event took place. Jewish writers considered him an archetypal man of prayer (4 Ezra 7:108; b. Sanhedrin 113a).

2. First Kings 18:1 places the events three years later rather than three and a half, but that was at the beginning of the Mount Carmel incident, and we don't know how much time ensued between that and the rainstorm of 18:45. It may be that "three and a half years" stems from Jewish tradition as a symbol of judgment (Dan 7:25; Rev 11:11; 12:14).

After Elijah's prayer for rain in 1 Kings 18:42, "the earth produced its crops," as James says. "Crops" is *karpos*, which alludes to James 5:7, the farmer waiting for rain when the land will "yield its valuable crop" at harvest time. This all looks back to the "good and perfect" gifts of 1:17 as well as to those who "sow in peace" and therefore "reap a harvest of righteousness" in 3:18. The message is clear: prayer works, and when God's people refuse to depend on self and live for the things of the world, turning to God in prayer, great things happen.

Once again, this is not a promise that we can get anything we want from God. In the all-embracing promise of John 14:12–14 Jesus says twice, "You may ask me for anything in my name, and I will do it." However, the key is "in my name." This prayer promise is for those who pray according to the will of God (see on 5:15a and the discussion of Rom 8:26). However, the message is completely positive here—prayer is wondrously effective and at the heart of the deep Christian life. It is the active outworking of our reliance on the Lord.

RESTORE THOSE WHO WANDER FROM THE FAITH (5:19-20)

This is a very unusual ending for a letter. James jettisons the normal conclusion with a benediction and closing greeting, undoubtedly due to the serious issues in his churches. Clearly he considers many in his churches to be in serious danger, and the phrase "wander from the truth" almost certainly sums up the sins of the letter. Sin is not to be trifled with, for the consequences are too great. I agree with those who consider this an extremely serious warning regarding the danger of apostasy and not just backsliding. It is the most serious situation possible.

This is closely connected with the corporate command of 5:16 regarding confession of sins and implies a responsibility that God's people have to watch over one another and rescue those who are falling astray. This mutual involvement in each other's lives is part of a restorative process. The letter itself is part of that process, as James wants to rescue his people from the sins noted throughout. This is another clause stressing the possibility (*ean*) of serious spiritual failure. "Wander" (*planēthē*) could be passive (led astray by a false teacher) or middle (go astray of one's own accord). The middle is by far the more likely, for nowhere are false prophets or teachers mentioned, and this basically sums up the ethical sins of the letter.

"The truth" is not just doctrinal error, for the issues throughout have to do with ethical conduct. While James certainly includes the gospel in his letter, he stresses the ethical aspects of it. He is talking about falling away from the whole gospel from the standpoint of both hearing (our knowledge) and doing (our praxis). I agree with the majority that the wandering James mentions connotes apostasy, not just backsliding, as in Hebrews 6:4-6; 10:26-27; 2 Peter 2:20-21; 1 John 5:16-17. They are wandering astray and deceived by serious sin (Matt 22:29; 2 Tim 3:13; 4:4; us 3:3; 2 Pet 2:15; Rev 2:20; 12:9; 13:14; 20:3, 8, 10).

The restoration occurs when "someone should bring that person back," returning them to their faith in Christ (knowing) and their walk with God (doing). It could be said that the Bible as a whole is a chronicle of restoration, for the Jewish people tended to fall into idolatry and error seemingly every other generation, leading to the exile under the Babylonians and the destruction of Jerusalem under the Romans. There is a frequent emphasis on returning the sinner to Christ throughout the New Testament (Rom 14:1–15:13; Gal 6:1–2; Eph 4:11–16; Phil 2:1–3, 14–18; Heb 4:1; 1 Pet 4:8).

Verse 19 looks at the basic problem from the standpoint of the sinner who is falling away. Verse 20 looks at it from the vantage point of the rescuer who brings them back to the Lord. "Remember this" in the NIV sounds like it is addressing the church ("brothers and sisters," v. 19) as a whole, but more likely James has in mind those who will restore the errant member. He wants them to "know" (ginōsketō, present tense to stress an ongoing realization) the significance of their duty to the apostate.

Their task is to turn the "sinner from the error of their way," depicting the Christian life as a pilgrimage or journey, with sinners straying off God's path into a dangerous ditch and the restorer rescuing them and getting them back on the correct path. The picture is similar to Christ's parable about the wide and narrow gate, when Jesus said, "For wide is the gate and broad is the road that leads to destruction" (Matt 7:13). Every person has to choose which path they will take in life. James considers this choice from the perspective of corporate responsibility to each other for these choices. As in Hebrews 12:12–13, we need each other to "strengthen your feeble arms and weak knees … so that the lame may not be disabled, but rather healed." Those crippled by sin and about to fall in the ditch need stronger believers to rescue and help them back on the straight path.

The result of this rescue operation is twofold (5:20). First, the restoration process "will save them from death," which in Greek reads literally, "save their soul from death" (*sōsei psychēn autou*), important because some read this as rescue from physical death (*sōzō* in 5:15). This could then be interpreted as akin to 1 Corinthians 11:29–30, where God took the lives of those who had treated the Lord's Supper unworthily. In this case it would be God taking the life of a shallow Christian before they can commit apostasy. That is highly improbable here. It is the "soul" saved from death, and this language throughout Scripture always speaks of spiritual death and eternal separation from God. They were headed for eternal punishment but have been rescued and given life.

There is one other area of uncertainty in this passage. The Greek has "save *their* soul," and it is possible to read this as saying the person restoring the sinner is the antecedent of "their" rather than the sinner. While possible, this is also highly unlikely, for the focus is on the people being restored to their walk with God more than those who rescue them in this context. "Their" (*autou*) occurs twice in five words, and the first time is "from the error of *their* ways," a clear reference to the sinner. It is highly likely that the second use also applies to the sinner.

Second, the restoration of the sinner will "cover over a multitude of sins," a clear reference to forgiveness as the result of repentance. Several passages lie behind this, like Psalm 32:1 ("Blessed is the one whose transgressions are forgiven, whose sins are covered") and Proverbs 10:12 ("love covers over all wrongs"). First Peter 4:8 is parallel: "love covers over a multitude of sins." The idea of covering over sins is behind the imagery of atonement, picturing God placing our sins under the mercy seat of the ark, his throne, so they are "covered" by it (Lev 17:11). A former believer who falls away has accumulated a "multitude" of unforgiven sins, and when they return to Christ these sins are forgiven, "covered" by the blood of Christ, and they are "saved."

———

This closing section of the book continues the diatribe on ethical
sins throughout this letter. These are three further areas in which
the tongue must be placed under God's control and used to glorify
him. The first (5:12) deals with oath-taking and demands honesty
and integrity in making claims and promises. Rather than deceiv-
ing people by a shallow vow to hide your lack of trustworthiness
in giving your word, you should be known as a person people can
rely on to keep promises.

The second example of a proper speech ethic is prayer and its
relation to physical illness (vv. 13-18). James begins by enumerat-
ing the ways we react to the trials and triumphs of life (vv. 13-14a).
Those who are in trouble will pray, and those who are happy with
the way things are going will praise God for the blessings that
have come their way. Notice that in both cases the attention is on
God and our relation to him, not just on the vicissitudes of life.
Then James turns to physical illness, which will be the focus of
the ensuing verses.

Three aspects of the proper reaction to illness are highlighted
here. First, James stresses the physical side (vv. 14b-15a), then the
spiritual side (15b-16a), and finally the power of true prayer to
accomplish things (16b-18). In any healing context both the physical and the spiritual must be addressed. They are inextricably
linked, for even the physical side of the solution, the anointing
with oil, is symbolic of the spiritual, as it is done "in the name of
the Lord." The medicinal olive oil depicts the spiritual surrender
of the person to the Lord and his healing presence. As an elder in
my church, I have often participated in anointing the sick with
oil, and every time in doing so we are handing the person over
to God and his healing presence. When we anoint them, we are
not demanding that God physically heal them but trusting in his
compassionate will for the person and their situation. God's "no"

or "wait" is a true answer to prayer, for he is giving to us and the sick person what is best in the situation.

Second, it is critical that the spiritual state of the church as a whole be centered on God. The command to "confess your sins to each other" (v. 16a) should not be narrowed to the sins that may have led to the illness. It is meant generally, for the spiritual depth of the church matters in the healing situation. When I bring my own illness to the church for prayer, my hope is that they will be praying for me from the perspective of a deep walk with God as a congregation. Corporate prayer is a powerful weapon against Satan and difficult situations like illness, but the spiritual state of the congregation makes a difference in prayer situations. From this standpoint, the church *at all times* should be working on their walk with God by confessing and praying and confessing together as the body of Christ, thereby continuing to grow in him as the community of Christ.

Third, James wants his churches to understand the power and effectiveness of a community that is doing just this (vv. 16b–18), for their prayer life will reflect their spiritual state in Christ. He begins by acknowledging the fact that we are all finite and prone to failure, just as was Elijah himself, the greatest of the miracle-working prophets. For all his power and effectiveness, he still ran for his life from little Queen Jezebel rather than trusting in God to remove her from the scene. In the same way, we fail often in our Christian walk but still can trust in the Lord and see wondrous things accomplished through us. All we need to do is place ourselves fully under God and trust in him, and the same prayer power that Elijah demonstrated can be ours.

The final section of this letter centers on the process of spiritual restoration in the church (vv. 19–20), and it encompasses all the ethical sins of the letter from the standpoint of the potential they all pose for tempting us and leading us away from Christ. As I stated above, the problem is with loss of salvation—apostasy, not just backsliding. In 5:16 James commands his readers to "confess your sins to each other," challenging weak Christians of the great danger of wandering away from God and his truths. At all times we should care enough about each other to admonish those whose faith is weak. This is a constant process and not just an occasional thing in the church. I am always struggling against the temptation of 1:12–15, and I need the help of my brothers and sisters in my church family in this process. Their responsibility is to bring me back to Christ and place me once more on the narrow path to God.

This restoration will accomplish two things, together the most important things that can happen to a human being during their earthly life. First, they will be saved from (eternal) death. When they wandered away and committed apostasy, they became non-Christians and were headed for final judgment and eternal condemnation. They had rejected Christ and lost everything, and as a result their future constituted a horror beyond belief. The person who brings them back to the Lord has become a tool of Christ the Savior and renewed their eternal hope, the greatest gift that can be given to another human being.

Second, and at the same time, all of the accumulated sins that were going to send these sinners to eternal hellfire have now been "covered" or been "atoned for" (see above), and the result is they have all been forgiven by God. Every sin that was leading them to eternal judgment in the lake of fire is now under the blood of Christ and covered by God's mercy seat, gone forever. There can be no more wondrous truth than this, and those who have brought this sinner back from the abyss should rejoice at the privilege of being the God-given and Spirit-empowered means of doing so.

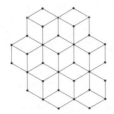

GLOSSARY

apocalyptic Refers to truths about God's plans for history that he has hidden in past generations but has revealed (the Greek *apokalypsis* means "unveiling") to his people. The name also describes a genre of ancient literature (including Revelation and parts of Daniel) that communicates these truths using vivid symbolism.

chiasm (n.), chiastic (adj.) A stylistic device in which a passage is organized into two sections, with the contents of the statements in the first half repeated in reverse order in the second half (ABC:C′B′A′).

christological (adj.), Christology (n.) Refers to the New Testament's presentation of the person and work of Christ, especially his identity as Messiah.

diaspora (n.), diasporic (adj.) Refers to the (often Greek-speaking) communities of Jews living outside Israel. The term comes from the Greek word for "scattering."

eschatological (adj.), eschatology (n.) Refers to the last things or the end times. Within this broad category, biblical scholars and theologians have identified more specific concepts. For instance, "realized eschatology" emphasizes the present work of Christ in the world as he prepares for the end of history. In "inaugurated eschatology," the last days have already begun but have not yet been consummated at the return of Christ.

eschaton Greek for "end" or "last," referring to the return of Christ and the end of history.

gnostic (adj.), Gnosticism (n.) Refers to the belief that special knowledge (Greek: *gnōsis*) is the basis of salvation. As a result of this heretical teaching, which developed in several forms in the early centuries AD, many gnostics held a negative view of the physical world.

Hellenism (n.), Hellenistic (adj.) Relates to the spread of Greek culture in the Mediterranean world after the conquests of Alexander the Great (356–323 BC).

inclusio A framing device in which the same word or phrase occurs at both the beginning and the end of a section of text.

Judaizers Label commonly used to identify a group of teachers who, in contradiction to Paul's gospel, encouraged Gentile Christians to observe the Jewish law and undergo the rite of circumcision. (The term "Judaizers" itself does not appear in the Bible.)

lex talionis Latin for "law of retaliation." This is the principle that those who have done some wrong will be punished in a similar degree and kind.

midrash (n.), midrashic (adj.) A Jewish exposition of a text using the techniques of ancient rabbis to give a detailed analysis of its meaning and theology.

parousia The event of Christ's second coming. The Greek word *parousia* means "arrival" or "presence."

Qumran A site near the northwest corner of the Dead Sea where a collection of scrolls (called the Dead Sea Scrolls) was found beginning in the 1940s. The community that lived at this site and wrote these scrolls separated themselves from the rest of Jewish society. Many scholars believe they were a branch of the Essenes, one of the three major Jewish sects mentioned by Josephus (*Antiquities* 13.171–72). The Dead Sea

Scrolls include manuscripts of Old Testament books as well
as other writings that are not part of Scripture. They do not
refer to Christianity, but do shed light on aspects of Judaism
around the time of Jesus.

Septuagint An ancient Greek translation of the Old Testament
that was used extensively in the early church.

Shekinah A word derived from the Hebrew *shakan* (to dwell), used
to describe God's personal presence taking the form of a
cloud, often in the context of the tabernacle or temple (e.g.,
Exod 40:38; Num 9:15; 1 Kgs 8:10–11).

soteriological (adj.), soteriology (n.) Relating to the doctrine of
salvation (Greek: *sōtēria*), including such subjects as atonement, justification, and sanctification.

typological (adj.), typology (n.) A literary device in which Old
Testament persons or events are the types that correspond
to and are fulfilled in New Testament realities.

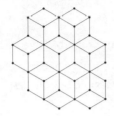

BIBLIOGRAPHY

Adamson, James B. *The Epistle of James.* New International Commentary on the New Testament. Grand Rapids: Eerdmans, 1976.

Bauckham, Richard. *James.* New Testament Readings. London: Routledge, 1999.

Blomberg, Craig L., and Mariam J. Kamell. *James.* Zondervan Exegetical Commentary on the New Testament. Grand Rapids: Zondervan, 2008.

Calvin, John. *Commentary on the Catholic Epistles.* Grand Rapids: Eerdmans, 1948 (original 1551).

Davids, Peter H. *The Epistle of James.* New International Greek Testament Commentary. Grand Rapids: Eerdmans, 1982.

Dibelius, Martin. *James.* Hermeneia. Philadelphia: Fortress, 1975.

Doriani, Daniel M. *James.* Reformed Expository Commentary. Phillipsburg, NJ: P&R, 2007.

Guthrie, George H. "James." In *The Expositor's Bible Commentary: Hebrews-Revelation*, edited by Tremper Longman III and David E. Garland, 13:197–274. Rev. ed. Grand Rapids: Zondervan, 2006.

Hartin, Patrick J. *James.* Sacra Pagina. Collegeville, MN: Liturgical Press, 2003.

Hiebert, D. Edmond. *The Epistle of James: Tests of a Living Faith*. Chicago: Moody Publishers, 1979.

Johnson, Luke Timothy. *The Letter of James*. Anchor Bible. New York: Doubleday, 1995.

Kistemaker, Simon J. *Exposition of the Epistle of James and the Epistles of John*. Grand Rapids: Baker, 1986.

Laws, Sophie. *A Commentary on the Epistle of James*. San Francisco: Harper & Row, 1980.

Martin, Ralph P. *James*. Word Biblical Commentary. Waco, TX: Word, 1988.

McCartney, Dan G. *James*. Baker Exegetical Commentary on the New Testament. Grand Rapids: Baker Academic, 2009.

McKnight, Scot. *The Letter of James*. New International Commentary on the New Testament. Grand Rapids: Eerdmans, 2011.

Moo, Douglas J. *The Letter of James*. Pillar New Testament Commentary. Grand Rapids: Eerdmans, 2000.

Motyer, J. Alec., *The Message of James*. Bible Speaks Today. Downers Grove, IL: InterVarsity Press, 1985.

Nystrom, David. *James*. NIV Application Commentary. Grand Rapids: Zondervan, 1997.

Richardson, Kurt A. *James*. New American Commentary. Nashville: Broadman & Holman, 1997.

Stulac, George M. *James*. IVP New Testament Commentary. Downers Grove, IL: InterVarsity Press, 1990.

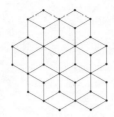

SUBJECT AND AUTHOR INDEX

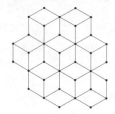

INDEX OF SCRIPTURE AND OTHER ANCIENT LITERATURE

Deuterocanonical Works

Old Testament Pseudepigrapha

Talmud and Related Literature

Other Rabbinic Works

Apostolic Fathers

Other Ancient Literature

Printed in the United States
By Bookmasters